The Best of the World's Classics

VOL. X

AMERICA—II

1807—1909

POE

LOWELL

LONGFELLOW

PARKMAN

THE BEST
OF THE
WORLD'S
CLASSICS

RESTRICTED
TO PROSE

HENRY CABOT LODGE
EDITOR-IN-CHIEF

FRANCIS W. HALSEY
ASSOCIATE EDITOR

With an Introduction, Biographical and Explanatory
Notes, etc.

IN TEN VOLUMES

Vol. X
AMERICA — II
INDEX

FUNK & WAGNALLS COMPANY
NEW YORK AND LONDON

CONTENTS

vi

CONTENTS

VOL. X—AMERICA—II

CONTENTS

CONTENTS

CONTENTS

CONTENTS

VOL. X

AMERICA—II

1807—1909

HENRY WADSWORTH LONGFELLOW

Born in 1807, died in 1882; graduated from Bowdoin in
1825; traveled in Europe in 1826-29; professor at Bowdoin
in 1829-35; again visited Europe in 1835-36; professor
at Harvard in 1836-54; published "Voices of the Night" in
1839, "Evangeline" in 1847, "Hiawatha" in 1855, "Miles
Standish" in 1858; "Tales of a Wayside Inn" in 1863, a
translation of Dante in 1867-70, "The Divine Tragedy" in
1871, and many other volumes of verse; his prose writings
include "Outre-Mer," published in 1835, and two novels,
"Hyperion," published in 1839, and "Kavanagh," in 1849.

MUSINGS IN PÈRE LACHAISE [1]

THE cemetery of Père Lachaise is the West-
minster Abbey of Paris. Both are the dwellings
of the dead; but in one they repose in green
alleys and beneath the open sky—in the other
their resting place is in the shadowy aisle and
beneath the dim arches of an ancient abbey. One
is a temple of nature; the other a temple of
art. In one the soft melancholy of the scene is
rendered still more touching by the warble of
birds and the shade of trees, and the grave receives the gentle visit of the sunshine and the
shower: in the other no sound but the passing
footfall breaks the silence of the place; the
twilight steals in through high and dusky windows; and the damps of the gloomy vault lie
heavy on the heart, and leave their stain upon
the moldering tracery of the tomb.

[1] From "Outre-Mer."

Père Lachaise stands just beyond the Barrière d'Aulney, on a hillside looking toward the city. Numerous gravel walks, winding through shady avenues and between marble monuments, lead up from the principal entrance to a chapel on the summit. There is hardly a grave that has not its little enclosure planted with shrubbery, and a thick mass of foliage half conceals each funeral stone. The sighing of the wind, as the branches rise and fall upon it—the occasional note of a bird among the trees, and the shifting of light and shade upon the tombs beneath have a soothing effect upon the mind; and I doubt whether any one can enter that enclosure, where repose the dust and ashes of so many great and good men, without feeling the religion of the place steal over him, and seeing something of the dark and gloomy expression pass off from the stern countenance of Death.

It was near the close of a bright summer afternoon that I visited this celebrated spot for the first time. The first object that arrested my attention on entering was a monument in the form of a small Gothic chapel which stands near the entrance, in the avenue leading to the right hand. On the marble couch within are stretched two figures, carved in stone and drest in the antique garb of the Middle Ages. It is the tomb of Abélard and Héloïse. The history of these two unfortunate lovers is too well known to need recapitulation; but perhaps it is not so well known how often their ashes were disturbed in the slumber of the grave. Abélard died in the monastery of St. Marcel, and was buried in the vaults of the church. His body was afterward removed to the convent of the Paraclete, at the request of Héloïse, and at her death her body was deposited in the same tomb. Three centuries they reposed together; after which they were separated to different sides of the church, to calm the delicate scruples of the lady abbess of the convent. More than a century afterward they were again united in the same tomb; and when at length the Paraclete was destroyed, their moldering remains were transported to the church of Nogent-sur-Seine. They were next deposited in an ancient cloister at Paris, and now repose near the gateway of the cemetery of Père Lachaise. What a singular destiny was theirs! that, after a life of such passionate and disastrous love—such sorrows, and tears, and penitence—their very dust should not be suffered to rest quietly in the grave!—that their death should so much resemble their life in its changes and vicissitudes, its partings and its meetings, its inquietudes and its persecutions!—that mistaken zeal should follow them down to the very tomb—as if earthly passion could glimmer, like a funeral lamp, amid the damps of the charnel house, and "even in their ashes burn their wonted fires"!

As I gazed on the sculptured forms before me, and the little chapel whose Gothic roof seemed to protect their marble sleep, my busy memory swung back the dark portals of the past, and the picture of their sad and eventful lives came up before me in the gloomy distance. What a lesson for those who are endowed with the fatal gift of genius! It would seem, indeed, that He who "tempers the wind to the shorn lamb" tempers also His chastisements to the errors and infirmities of a weak and simple mind—while the transgressions of him upon whose nature are more strongly marked the intellectual attributes of the Deity are followed, even upon earth, by severer tokens of the Divine displeasure. He who sins in the darkness of a benighted intellect sees not so clearly, through the shadows that surround him, the countenance of an offended God; but he who sins in the broad noonday of a clear and radiant mind, when at length the delirium of sensual passion has subsided and the cloud flits away from before the sun, trembles beneath the searching eye of that accusing Power which is strong in the strength of a godlike intellect. Thus the mind and the heart are closely linked together, and the errors of genius bear with them their own chastisement, even upon earth. The history of Abélard and Héloïse is an illustration of this truth. But at length they sleep well. Their lives are like a tale that is told; their errors are "folded up like a book"; and what mortal hand shall break the seal that death has set upon them?

Leaving this interesting tomb behind me, I took a pathway to the left, which conducted me up the hillside. I soon found myself in the deep shade of heavy foliage, where the branches of the yew and willow mingled, interwoven with the tendrils and blossoms of the honeysuckle. I now stood in the most populous part of this city of tombs. Every step awakened a new train of thrilling recollections, for at every step my eye caught the name of some one whose glory had exalted the character of his native land, and resounded across the waters of the Atlantic.

Philosophers, historians, musicians, warriors, and poets slept side by side around me; some beneath the gorgeous monument, and some beneath the simple headstone. But the political intrigue, the dream of science, the historical research, the ravishing harmony of sound, the tried courage, the inspiration of the lyre — where are they? With the living, and not with the dead! The right hand has lost its cunning in the grave; but the soul, whose high volitions it obeyed, still lives to reproduce itself in ages yet to come.

Amid these graves of genius I observed here and there a splendid monument, which had been raised by the pride of family over the dust of men who could lay no claim either to the gratitude or remembrance of posterity. Their presence seemed like an intrusion into the sanctuary of genius. What had wealth to do there? Why should it crowd the dust of the great? That was no thoroughfare of business—no mart of gain! There were no costly banquets there; no silken garments, nor gaudy liveries, nor obsequious attendants! "What servants," says Jeremy Taylor, "shall we have to wait upon us in the grave? what friends to visit us? what officious people to cleanse away the moist and unwholesome cloud reflected upon our faces from the sides of the weeping vaults, which are the longest weepers for our funerals?" Material wealth gives a factitious superiority to the living, but the treasures of intellect give a real superiority to the dead; and the rich man, who would not deign to walk the street with the starving and penniless man of genius, deems it an honor, when death has redeemed the fame of the neglected, to have his ashes laid beside him, and to claim with him the silent companionship of the grave.

I continued my walk through the numerous winding paths, as chance or curiosity directed me. Now I was lost in a little green hollow overhung with thick-leaved shrubbery, and then came out upon an elevation, from which, through an opening in the trees, the eye caught glimpses of the city, and the little esplanade at the foot of the hill where the poor lie buried. There poverty hires its grave and takes but a short lease of the narrow house. At the end of a few months, or at most of a few years, the tenant is dislodged to give place to another, and he in turn to a third. "Who," says Sir Thomas Browne, "knows the fate of his bones, or how often he is to be buried? Who hath the oracle of his ashes, or whither they are to be scattered?"

Yet even in that neglected corner the hand of affection had been busy in decorating the hired house. Most of the graves were surrounded with a slight wooden paling, to secure them from the passing footstep; there was hardly one so deserted as not to be marked with its little wooden cross and decorated with a garland of flowers; and here and there I could perceive a solitary mourner, clothed in black, stooping to plant a shrub on the grave, or sitting in motionless sorrow beside it.

As I passed on amid the shadowy avenues of the cemetery, I could not help comparing my own impressions with those which others have felt when walking alone among the dwellings of the dead. Are, then, the sculptured urn and storied monument nothing more than symbols of family pride? Is all I see around me a memorial of the living more than of the dead, an empty show of sorrow, which thus vaunts itself in mournful pageant and funeral parade? Is it indeed true, as some have said, that the simple wild flower which springs spontaneously upon the grave, and the rose which the hand of affection plants there, are fitter objects wherewith to adorn the narrow house? No! I feel that it is not so! Let the good and the great be honored even in the grave. Let the sculptured marble direct our footsteps to the scene of their long sleep; let the chiseled epitaph repeat their names, and tell us where repose the nobly good and wise! It is not true that all are equal in the grave. There is no equality even there. The mere handful of dust and ashes, the mere distinction of prince and beggar, of a rich winding sheet and a shroudless burial, of a solitary grave and a family vault— were this all, then, indeed it would be true that death is a common leveler. Such paltry distinctions as those of wealth and poverty are soon leveled by the spade and mattock, the damp breath of the grave blots them out forever. But there are other distinctions which even the mace of death can not level or obliterate. Can it break down the distinction of virtue and vice? Can it confound the good with the bad? the noble with the base? all that is truly great, and pure, and godlike, with all that is scorned, and sinful, and degraded? No! Then death is not a common leveler! . . .

Before I left the graveyard the shades of

evening had fallen, and the objects around me grown dim and indistinct. As I passed the gateway, I turned to take a parting look. I could distinguish only the chapel on the summit of the hill, and here and there a lofty obelisk of snow-white marble, rising from the black and heavy mass of foliage around, and pointing upward to the gleam of the departed sun, that still lingered in the sky, and mingled with the soft starlight of a summer evening.

EDGAR ALLAN POE

Born in 1809, died in 1849; his father and mother actors; adopted by John Allan of Richmond after his mother's death; educated in Richmond, in England, at the University of Virginia, and at West Point; published "Tamerlane" in 1827; settled in Baltimore and devoted himself to literature; editor of several magazines 1835-44; published "The Raven" in 1845, "Al Aaraaf" in 1829, "Tales of the Grotesque and Arabesque" in 1840.

I

THE CASK OF AMONTILLADO [1]

It was about dusk, one evening during the supreme madness of the carnival season, that I encountered my friend. He accosted me with excessive warmth, for he had been drinking much. The man wore motley. He had on a tight-fitting parti-striped dress, and his head was surmounted by the conical cap and bells. I was so pleased to see him that I thought I should never have done wringing his hand.

I said to him: "My dear Fortunato, you are luckily met. How remarkable well you are looking to-day! But I have received a pipe of what passes for Amontillado, and I have my doubts."

"How?" said he. "Amontillado? A pipe? Impossible! And in the middle of the carnival!"

"I have my doubts," I replied; "and I was silly enough to pay the full Amontillado price

[1] Published in *Godey's Magazine* in 1846.

11

without consulting you in the matter. You were not to be found, and I was fearful of losing a bargain."

"Amontillado!"

"I have my doubts—"

"Amontillado!"

"And I must satisfy them."

"Amontillado!"

"As you are engaged, I am on my way to Luchesi. If any one has a critical turn, it is he. He will tell me—"

"Luchesi can not tell Amontillado from Sherry."

"And yet some fools will have it that his taste is a match for your own."

"Come, let us go."

"Whither?"

"To your vaults."

"My friend, no; I will not impose upon your good nature. I perceive you have an engagement. Luchesi—"

"I have no engagement; come."

"My friend, no. It is not the engagement, but the severe cold with which I perceive you are afflicted. The vaults are insufferably damp. They are encrusted with niter."

"Let us go, nevertheless. The cold is merely nothing. Amontillado! You have been imposed upon. And as for Luchèsi, he can not distinguish Sherry from Amontillado."

Thus speaking, Fortunato possest himself of my arm. Putting on a mask of black silk, and drawing a *roquelaure* closely about my person, I suffered him to hurry me to my palazzo.

There were no attendants at home; they had

absconded to make merry in honor of the time. I had told them that I should not return until the morning, and had given them explicit orders not to stir from the house. These orders were sufficient, I well knew, to insure their immediate disappearance, one and all, as soon as my back was turned.

I took from their sconces two flambeaux, and giving one to Fortunato, bowed him through several suites of rooms to the archway that led into the vaults. I passed down a long and winding staircase, requesting him to be cautious as he followed. We came at length to the foot of the descent, and stood together on the damp ground of the catacombs of the Montresors.

The gait of my friend was unsteady, and the bells upon his cap jingled as he strode.

"The pipe," said he.

"It is farther on," said I; "but observe the white web-work which gleams from these cavern walls."

He turned toward me, and looked into my eyes with two filmy orbs that distilled the rheum of intoxication.

"Niter?" he asked, at length.

"Niter," I replied. "How long have you had that cough?"

"Ugh! ugh! ugh—ugh! ugh! ugh!—ugh! ugh! ugh!—ugh! ugh! ugh!—ugh! ugh! ugh!"

My poor friend found it impossible to reply for many minutes.

"It is nothing," he said, at last.

"Come," I said, with decision, "we will go back; your health is precious. You are rich, respected, admired, beloved; you are happy, as once I was. You are a man to be missed. For me it is no matter. We will go back; you will be ill, and I can not be responsible. Besides, there is Luchesi—"

"Enough," he said; "the cough is a mere nothing; it will not kill me. I shall not die."

"True—true," I replied; "and, indeed, I had no intention of alarming you unnecessarily—but you should use all proper caution. A draft of this Medoc will defend us from the damps."

Here I knocked off the neck of a bottle which I drew from a long row of its fellows that lay upon the mold.

"Drink," I said, presenting him the wine.

He raised it to his lips with a leer. He paused and nodded to me familiarly, while his bells jingled.

"I drink," he said, "to the buried that repose around us."

"And I to your long life."

He again took my arm, and we proceeded.

"These vaults," he said, "are extensive."

"The Montresors," I replied, "were a great and numerous family."

"I forget your arms."

"A huge human foot d'or; in a field azure; the foot crushes a serpent rampant whose fangs are imbedded in the heel."

"And the motto?"

"*Nemo me impune lacessit.*"

"Good!" he said.

The wine sparkled in his eyes and the bells jingled. My own fancy grew warm with the Medoc. We had passed through walls of piled bones, with casks and puncheons intermingling, into the inmost recesses of the catacombs. I paused again, and this time I made bold to seize Fortunato by an arm above the elbow.

"The niter!" I said; "see, it increases. It hangs like moss upon the vaults. We are below the river's bed. The drops of moisture trickle among the bones. Come, we will go back ere it is too late. Your cough—"

"It is nothing," he said; "let us go on. But first, another draft of the Medoc."

I broke and reached him a flagon of De Grave. He emptied it at a breath. His eyes flashed with a fierce light. He laughed and threw the bottle upward with a gesticulation I did not understand.

I looked at him in surprize. He repeated the movement—a grotesque one.

"You do not comprehend!" he said.

"Not I," I replied.

"Then you are not of the brotherhood."

"How?"

"You are not of the masons."

"Yes, yes," I said, "yes, yes."

"You? Impossible! A mason?"

"A mason," I replied.

"A sign," he said.

"It is this," I answered, producing a trowel from beneath the folds of my *roquelaure*.

"You jest," he exclaimed, recoiling a few paces. "But let us proceed to the Amontillado."

"Be it so," I said, replacing the tool beneath the cloak, and again offering him my arm. He leaned upon it heavily. We continued our route in search of the Amontillado. We passed through a range of low arches, descended, passed on, and descending again, arrived at a deep crypt, in which the foulness of the air caused our flambeaux rather to glow than flame.

At the most remote end of the crypt there appeared another less spacious. Its walls had been lined with human remains, piled to the vault overhead, in the fashion of the great catacombs of Paris. Three sides of this interior crypt were still ornamented in this manner. From the fourth the bones had been thrown down, and lay promiscuously upon the earth, forming at one point a mound of some size. Within the walls thus exposed by the displacing of the bones, we perceived a still interior recess, in depth about four feet, in width three, in height six or seven. It seemed to have been constructed for no special use within itself, but formed merely the interval between two of the colossal supports of the roof of the catacombs, and was backed by one of their circumscribing walls of solid granite.

It was in vain that Fortunato, uplifting his dull torch, endeavored to pry into the depth of the recess. Its termination the feeble light did not enable us to see.

"Proceed," I said, "herein is the Amontillado. As for Luchesi—"

"He is an ignoramus," interrupted my friend, as he stept unsteadily forward, while I followed immediately at his heels. In an instant he had reached the extremity of the niche, and finding his progress arrested by the rock, stood stupidly bewildered. A moment more and I had fettered him to the granite. In its surface were two iron staples, distant from each other about two feet, horizontally. From one of these depended a short chain, from the other a padlock. Throwing the links about his waist, it was but the work of a few seconds to secure it. He was too much astounded to resist. Withdrawing the key I stept back from the recess.

"Pass your hand," I said, "over the wall; you can not help feeling the niter. Indeed it is very damp. Once more let me implore you to return. No? Then I must positively leave you. But I must first render you all the little attentions in my power."

"The Amontillado!" ejaculated my friend, not yet recovered from his astonishment.

"True," I replied; "the Amontillado."

As I said these words I busied myself among the pile of bones of which I have before spoken. Throwing them aside, I soon uncovered a quantity of building stone and mortar. With these materials and with the aid of my trowel, I began vigorously to wall up the entrance of the niche.

I had scarcely laid the first tier of the masonry when I discovered that the intoxication of Fortunato had in a great measure worn off. The earliest indication I had of this was a low moaning cry from the depth of the recess. It was *not* the cry of a drunken man. There was then a long and obstinate silence. I laid the second tier, and the third, and the fourth; and then I heard the furious vibrations of the chain. The noise lasted for several minutes, during which, that I might harken to it with the more satisfaction, I ceased my labors and sat down upon the bones. When at last the clanking subsided, I resumed the trowel, and finished without interruption the fifth, the sixth, and the seventh tier. The wall was now nearly upon a level with my breast. I again paused, and holding the flambeaux over the mason-work, threw a few feeble rays upon the figure within.

A succession of loud and shrill screams, bursting suddenly from the throat of the chained form, seemed to thrust me violently back. For a brief moment I hesitated—I trembled. Unsheathing my rapier, I began to grope with it about the recess; but the thought of an instant reassured me. I placed my hand upon the solid fabric of the catacombs, and felt satisfied. I reapproached the wall. I replied to the yells of him who clamored. I reechoed—I aided—I surpassed them in volume and in strength. I did this, and the clamorer grew still.

It was now midnight, and my task was drawing to a close. I had completed the eighth, the ninth, and the tenth tier. I had finished a portion of the last and the eleventh; there remained but a single stone to be fitted and plastered in. I struggled with its weight; I placed it partially in its destined position. But now there came from out the niche a low laugh that erected the hairs upon my head. It was succeeded by a sad voice, which I had difficulty in recognizing as that of the noble Fortunato. The voice said:

"Ha! ha! ha!—he! he!—a very good joke—indeed—an excellent jest. We will have many a rich laugh about it at the palazzo—he! he! he!—over our wine—he! he! he!"

"The Amontillado!" I said.

"He! he! he!—he! he! he!—yes, the Amontillado. But is it not getting late? Will they not be awaiting us at the palazzo, the Lady Fortunato and the rest? Let us be gone."

"Yes," I said, "let us be gone."

"For the love of God, Montresor!"

"Yes," I said, "for the love of God!"

But to these words I harkened in vain for a reply. I grew impatient. I called aloud:

"Fortunato!"

No answer. I called again:

"Fortunato!"

No answer still. I thrust a torch through the remaining aperture and let it fall within. There came forth in return only a jingling of the bells. My heart grew sick—on account of the dampness of the catacombs. I hastened to make an end of my labor. I forced the last stone into its position; I plastered it up. Against the new masonry I reerected the old rampart of bones. For the half of a century no mortal has disturbed them. *In pace requiescat!*

II

OF HAWTHORNE AND THE SHORT STORY [2]

THE reputation of the author of "Twice-Told Tales" has been confined, until very lately, to literary society; and I have not been wrong, perhaps, in citing him as the example, par excel-

[2] From a review of Hawthorne's "Twice Told Tales" and "Mosses from an Old Manse," published in *Godey's Magazine* in 1846. Except for an earlier notice by Longfellow in *The North American Review*, this was the first notable recognition Hawthorne's stories received from a contemporary critic.

lence, in this country, of the privately admired
and publicly-unappreciated man of genius. Within the last year or two, it is true, an occasional
critic has been urged, by honest indignation, into
very warm approval. Mr. Webber,[3] for instance
(than whom no one has a keener relish for that
kind of writing which Mr. Hawthorne has best
illustrated), gave us, in a late number of *The
American Review*, a cordial and certainly a full
tribute to his talents; and since the issue of the
"Mosses from an Old Manse" criticisms of similar tone have been by no means infrequent in
our more authoritative journals. I can call to
mind few reviews of Hawthorne published before
the "Mosses." One I remember in *Arcturus*
(edited by Matthews and Duyckinck[4]) for May,
1841; another in the *American Monthly* (edited
by Hoffman[5] and Herbert) for March, 1838; a
third in the ninety-sixth number of *The North
American Review*. These criticisms, however,
seemed to have little effect on the popular taste
—at least, if we are to form any idea of the
popular taste by reference to its expression in
the newspapers, or by the sale of the author's
book. It was never the fashion (until lately)

---

[3] Charles Wilkens Webber, magazine writer and author
of a dozen books now forgotten, was a native of Kentucky
who settled in New York. In 1855 he joined William
Walker in his filibustering expedition to Central America,
and was killed in the battle of Rivas.

[4] Evert A. Duyckinck, joint editor with his brother of the
"Cyclopedia of American Literature."

[5] Charles Fenno Hoffman, poet, novelist, and critic, was
related to Mathilda Hoffman, the sweetheart of Washington
Irving.

to speak of him in any summary of our best authors. . . .

Beyond doubt, this inappreciation of him on the part of the public arose chiefly from the two causes to which I have referred—from the facts that he is neither a man of wealth nor a quack; but these are insufficient to account for the whole effect. No small portion of it is attributable to the very marked idiosyncrasy of Mr. Hawthorne himself. In one sense, and in great measure, to be peculiar is to be original, and than the true originality there is no higher literary virtue. This true or commendable originality, however, implies not the uniform, but the continuous peculiarity—a peculiarity springing from ever-active vigor of fancy—better still if from ever-present force of imagination, giving its own hue, its own character to everything it touches, and, especially, self-impelled to touch everything. . . .

The pieces in the volumes entitled "Twice-Told Tales" are now in their third republication, and, of course, are thrice-told. Moreover, they are by no means all tales, either in the ordinary or in the legitimate understanding of the term. Many of them are pure essays. Of the Essays I must be content to speak in brief. They are each and all beautiful, without being characterized by the polish and adaptation so visible in the tales proper. A painter would at once note their leading or predominant feature, and style it repose. There is no attempt at effect. All is quiet, thoughtful, subdued. Yet this repose may exist simultaneously with high originality of thought; and Mr. Hawthorne has demonstrated

21

the fact. At every turn we meet with novel combinations; yet these combinations never surpass the limits of the quiet. We are soothed as we read; and withal is a calm astonishment that ideas so apparently obvious have never occurred or been presented to us before. Herein our author differs materially from Lamb or Hunt or Hazlitt—who, with vivid originality of manner and expression, have less of the true novelty of thought than is generally supposed, and whose originality, at best, has an uneasy and meretricious quaintness, replete with startling effects unfounded in nature, and inducing trains of reflection which lead to no satisfactory result. The essays of Hawthorne have much of the character of Irving, with more of originality, and less of finish; while, compared with the *Spectator*, they have a vast superiority at all points. The *Spectator*, Mr. Irving and Hawthorne have in common that tranquil and subdued manner which I have chosen to denominate repose; but, in the case of the two former, this repose is attained rather by the absence of novel combination, or of originality, than otherwise, and consists chiefly in the calm, quiet, unostentatious expression of commonplace thoughts, in an unambitious, unadulterated Saxon. In them, by strong effort, we are made to conceive the absence of all. In the essays before me the absence of effort is too obvious to be mistaken, and a strong undercurrent of suggestion runs continuously beneath the upper stream of the tranquil thesis. In short, these effusions of Mr. Hawthorne are the product of a truly imaginative intellect, restrained, and in some measure represt by fastidiousness of taste, by constitutional melancholy, and by indolence.

But it is of his tales that I desire principally to speak. The tale proper, in my opinion, affords unquestionably the fairest field for the exercise of the loftiest talent which can be afforded by the wide domains of mere prose. Were I bidden to say how the highest genius could be most advantageously employed for the best display of its own powers, I should answer, without hesitation—in the composition of a rimed poem, not to exceed in length what might be perused in an hour. Within this limit alone can the highest order of true poetry exist. I need only here say, upon this topic, that, in almost all classes of composition, the unity of effect or impression is a point of the greatest importance. It is clear, moreover, that this unity can not be thoroughly preserved in productions whose perusal can not be completed at one sitting. We may continue the reading of a prose composition, from the very nature of prose itself, much longer than we can persevere, to any good purpose, in the perusal of a poem. This latter, if truly fulfilling the demands of the poetic sentiment, induces an exaltation of the soul which can not be long sustained. All high excitements are necessarily transient. Thus a long poem is a paradox. And, without unity of impression, the deepest effects can not be brought about. Epics were the offspring of an imperfect sense of art, and their reign is no more. A poem too brief may produce a vivid, but never an intense or enduring impression. Without a certain continuity of effort —without a certain duration or repetition of purpose—the soul is never deeply moved. There must be the dropping of the water upon the rock. De Béranger has wrought brilliant things—pungent and spirit-stirring—but, like all impassive bodies, they lack momentum, and thus fail to satisfy the poetic sentiment. They sparkle and excite, but, from want of continuity, fail deeply to impress. Extreme brevity will degenerate into epigrammatism; but the sin of extreme length is even more unpardonable. *In medio tutissimus ibis.* Were I called upon, however, to designate that class of composition which, next to such a poem as I have suggested, should best fulfil the demands of high genius—should offer it the most advantageous field of exertion—I should unhesitatingly speak of the prose tale, as Mr. Hawthorne has here exemplified it. I allude to the short prose narrative, requiring from a half-hour to one or two hours in its perusal.

Of Mr. Hawthorne's "Tales" we would say, emphatically that they belong to the highest region of art—an art subservient to genius of a very lofty order. . . . We know of few compositions which the critic can more honestly commend than these "Twice-Told Tales." As Americans, we feel proud of the book.

Mr. Hawthorne's distinctive trait is invention, creation, imagination, originality—a trait which, in the literature of fiction, is positively worth all the rest. But the nature of the originality, so far as regards its manifestation in letters, is but imperfectly understood. The inventive or original mind as frequently displays itself in novelty of tone as in novelty of matter. Mr. Hawthorne is original in all points. It would be a matter of some difficulty to designate the best of these tales; we repeat that, without exception, they are beautiful.

He has the purest style, the finest taste, the most available scholarship, the most delicate humor, the most touching pathos, the most radiant imagination, the most consummate ingenuity; and with these varied good qualities he has done well as a mystic. But is there any one of these qualities which should prevent his doing doubly as well in a career of honest, upright, sensible, prehensible and comprehensible things? Let him mend his pen, get a bottle of visible ink, come out from the "Old Manse," cut Mr. Alcott, hang (if possible) the editor of *The Dial*, and throw out of the window to the pigs all his odd numbers of *The North American Review*.

III

OF WILLIS, BRYANT, HALLECK, AND MACAULAY [6]

WHATEVER may be thought of Mr. Willis's talents, there can be no doubt about the fact that, both as an author and as a man, he has made a good deal of noise in the world—at least for an American. His literary life, in especial, has been one continual emeute; but then his literary character is modified or impelled in a

[6] Passages selected from articles now printed in Volume II of the "Works of Poe," as published in New York in 1876.

very remarkable degree by his personal one.
His success (for in point of fame, if of nothing
else, he has certainly been successful) is to be
attributed one-third to his mental ability and
two-thirds to his physical temperament—the latter goading him into the accomplishment of what
the former merely gave him the means of accom-
plishing. . . . At a very early age, Mr. Willis
seems to have arrived at an understanding that,
in a republic such as ours, the mere man of
letters must ever be a cipher, and endeavored,
accordingly, to unite the eclat of the litterateur
with that of the man of fashion or of society.
He "pushed himself," went much into the world,
made friends with the gentler sex, "delivered"
poetical addresses, wrote "scriptural" poems,
traveled, sought the intimacy of noted women,
and got into quarrels with notorious men. All
these things served his purpose—if, indeed, I
am right in supposing that he had any purpose
at all. It is quite probable that, as before hinted,
he acted only in accordance with his physical
temperament; but, be this as it may, his personal
greatly advanced, if it did not altogether establish his literary fame. I have often carefully considered whether, without the physique
of which I speak, there is that in the absolute
morale of Mr. Willis which would have earned
him reputation as a man of letters, and my
conclusion is that he could not have failed to
become noted in some degree under almost any
circumstances, but that about two-thirds (as
above stated) of his appreciation by the public
should be attributed to those adventures which
grew immediately out of his animal constitution.

Mr. Bryant's position in the poetical world is, perhaps, better settled than that of any American. There is less difference of opinion about his rank; but, as usual, the agreement is more decided in private literary circles than in what appears to be the public expression of sentiment as gleaned from the press. I may as well observe here, too, that this coincidence of opinion in private circles is in all cases very noticeable when compared with the discrepancy of the apparent public opinion. In private it is quite a rare thing to find any strongly-marked disagreement —I mean, of course, about mere autorial merit. . . . It will never do to claim for Bryant a genius of the loftiest order, but there has been latterly, since the days of Mr. Longfellow and Mr. Lowell, a growing disposition to deny him genius in any respect. He is now commonly spoken of as "a man of high poetical talent, very 'correct,' with a warm appreciation of the beauty of nature and great descriptive powers, but rather too much of the old-school manner of Cowper, Goldsmith and Young." This is the truth, but not the whole truth. Mr. Bryant has genius, and that of a marked character, but it has been overlooked by modern schools, because deficient in those externals which have become in a measure symbolical of those schools.

The name of Halleck is at least as well established in the poetical world as that of any American. Our principal poets are, perhaps, most frequently named in this order—Bryant, Halleck, Dana, Sprague,[7] Longfellow, Willis, and so on—

---

[7] Charles Sprague, born in Boston in 1791, was known in his own day as "the American Pope."

Halleck coming second in the series, but holding, in fact, a rank in the public opinion quite equal to that of Bryant. The accuracy of the arrangement as above made may, indeed, be questioned. For my own part, I should have it thus—Longfellow, Bryant, Halleck, Willis, Sprague, Dana; and, estimating rather the poetic capacity than the poems actually accomplished, there are three or four comparatively unknown writers whom I would place in the series between Bryant and Halleck, while there are about a dozen whom I should assign a position between Willis and Sprague. Two dozen at least might find room between Sprague and Dana—this latter, I fear, owing a very large portion of his reputation to his quondam editorial connection with *The North American Review*. One or two poets, now in my mind's eye, I should have no hesitation in posting above even Mr. Longfellow—still not intending this as very extravagant praise. . . . Mr. Halleck, in the apparent public estimate, maintains a somewhat better position than that to which, on absolute grounds, he is entitled. There is something, too, in the bonhomie of certain of his compositions—something altogether distinct from poetic merit—which has aided to establish him; and much also must be admitted on the score of his personal popularity, which is deservedly great. With all these allowances, however, there will still be found a large amount of poetical fame to which he is fairly entitled . . . Personally he is a man to be admired, respected, but more especially beloved. His address has all the captivating bonhomie which is the leading feature of his poetry, and, indeed, of his whole moral nature. With his friends he is all ardor, enthusiasm and cordiality, but to the world at large he is reserved, shunning society, into which he is seduced only with difficulty, and upon rare occasions. The love of solitude seems to have become with him a passion.

Macaulay has obtained a reputation which, altho deservedly great, is yet in a remarkable measure undeserved. The few who regard him merely as a terse, forcible and logical writer, full of thought, and abounding in original views, often sagacious and never otherwise than admirably exprest—appear to us precisely in the right. The many who look upon him as not only all this, but as a comprehensive and profound thinker, little prone to error, err essentially themselves. The source of the general mistake lies in a very singular consideration—yet in one upon which we do not remember ever to have heard a word of comment. We allude to a tendency in the public mind toward logic for logic's sake—a liability to confound the vehicle with the conveyed—an aptitude to be so dazzled by the luminousness with which an idea is set forth as to mistake it for the luminousness of the idea itself. The error is one exactly analogous with that which leads the immature poet to think himself sublime wherever he is obscure, because obscurity is a source of the sublime—thus confounding obscurity of expression with the expression of obscurity. In the case of Macaulay —and we may say, *en passant*, of our own Channing—we assent to what he says too often because we so very clearly understand what it is that he intends to say. Comprehending vividly the points and the sequence of his argument, we fancy that we are concurring in the argument itself. It is not every mind which is at once able to analyze the satisfaction it receives from such essays as we see here. If it were merely beauty of style for which they were distinguished —if they were remarkable only for rhetorical flourishes—we would not be apt to estimate these flourishes at more than their due value. We would not agree with the doctrines of the essayist on account of the elegance with which they were urged. On the contrary, we would be inclined to disbelief. But when all ornament save that of simplicity is disclaimed—when we are attacked by precision of language, by perfect accuracy of expression, by directness and singleness of thought, and above all by a logic the most rigorously close and consequential—it is hardly a matter for wonder that nine of us out of ten are content to rest in the gratification thus received as in the gratification of absolute truth.

OLIVER WENDELL HOLMES

Born in 1809, died in 1894; professor in the Medical School of Harvard in 1847-82; wrote for the *Atlantic Monthly* "The Autocrat of the Breakfast Table" in 1857-58, "The Professor at the Breakfast Table" in 1859, "The Poet at the Breakfast Table" in 1872; published "Elsie Venner" in 1861, "The Guardian Angel" in 1868, "A Mortal Antipathy" in 1885; a collection of verse entitled "Songs in Many Keys" in 1861, "Humorous Poems" in 1865, "Songs of Many Seasons," in 1874, "Before the Curfew" in 1888; also wrote volumes of essays and memoirs of Emerson and Motley.

I

OF DOCTORS, LAWYERS, AND MINISTERS [1]

"WHAT is your general estimate of doctors, lawyers, and ministers?" said I.

"Wait a minute, till I have got through with your first question," said the Master. "One thing at a time. You asked me about the young doctors, and about our young doctors, they come home *très bien chaussés*, as a Frenchman would say, mighty well shod with professional knowledge. But when they begin walking round among their poor patients—they don't commonly start with millionaires—they find that their new shoes

[1] From Chapter V of "The Poet at the Breakfast Table." Copyright, 1872, 1891, by Oliver Wendell Holmes. Published by Houghton, Mifflin Company.

of scientific acquirements have got to be broken in just like a pair of boots or brogans. I don't know that I have put it quite strong enough. Let me try again. You've seen those fellows at the circus that get up on horseback, so big that you wonder how they could climb into the saddle. But pretty soon they throw off their outside coat, and the next minute another one, and then the one under that, and so they keep peeling off one garment after another till people begin to look queer and think they are going too far for strict propriety. Well, that is the way a fellow with a real practical turn serves a good many of his scientific wrappers—flings 'em off for other people to pick up, and goes right at the work of curing stomach-aches and all the other little mean unscientific complaints that make up the larger part of every doctor's business. I think our Dr. Benjamin is a worthy young man, and if you are in need of a doctor at any time I hope you will go to him; and if you come off without harm, I will—recommend some other friend to try him.''

I thought he was going to say he would try him in his own person; but the Master is not fond of committing himself.

''Now I will answer your other question,'' he said. ''The lawyers are the cleverest men, the ministers are the most learned, and the doctors are the most sensible.''

''The lawyers are a picked lot, 'first scholars,' and the like, but their business is as unsympathetic as Jack Ketch's. There is nothing humanizing in their relations with their fellow creatures. They go for the side that retains them. They defend the man they know to be a rogue, and not very rarely throw suspicion on the man they know to be innocent. Mind you, I am not finding fault with them—every side of a case has a right to the best statement it admits of; but I say it does not tend to make them sympathetic. Suppose in a case of Fever *vs.* Patient, the doctor should side with either party according to whether the old miser or his expectant heir was his employer. Suppose the minister should side with the Lord or the devil, according to the salary offered, and other incidental advantages, where the soul of a sinner was in question. You can see what a piece of work it would make of their sympathies. But the lawyers are quicker witted than either of the other professions, and abler men generally. They are good-natured, or if they quarrel, their quarrels are above-board. I don't think they are as accomplished as the ministers; but they have a way of cramming with special knowledge for a case, which leaves a certain shallow sediment of intelligence in their memories about a good many things. They are apt to talk law in mixt company; and they have a way of looking round when they make a point, as if they were addressing a jury, that is mighty aggravating—as I once had occasion to see when one of 'em, and a pretty famous one, put me on the witness stand at a dinner party once.

"The ministers come next in point of talent. They are far more curious and widely interested outside of their own calling than either of the other professions. I like to talk with 'em. They are interesting men: full of good feelings, hard workers, always foremost in good deeds, and on the whole the most efficient civilizing class—working downward from knowledge to ignorance, that is; not so much upward, perhaps—that we have. The trouble is that so many of 'em work in harness, and it is pretty sure to chafe somewhere. They feed us on canned meats mostly. They cripple our instincts and reason, and give us a crutch of doctrine. I have talked with a great many of 'em, of all sorts of belief; and I don't think they are quite so easy in their minds, the greater number of them, nor so clear in their convictions as one would think to hear 'em lay down the law in the pulpit. They used to lead the intelligence of their parishes; now they do pretty well if they keep up with it, and they are very apt to lag behind it. Then they must have a colleague. The old minister thinks he can hold to his old course, sailing right into the wind's eye of human nature, as straight as that famous old skipper John Bunyan; the young minister falls off three or four points, and catches the breeze that left the old man's sails all shivering. By-and-by the congregation will get ahead of him, and then it must have another new skipper. The priest holds his own pretty well; the minister is coming down every generation nearer and nearer to the common level of the useful citizen—no oracle at all, but a man of more than average moral instincts, who, if he knows anything, knows how little he knows. The ministers are good talkers, only the struggle between nature and grace makes some of 'em a little awkward occasionally. The women do their best to spoil 'em, as they do the poets. You find it pleasant to be spoiled, no doubt; so do they. Now and then one of 'em goes over the dam; no wonder—they're always in the rapids.''

By this time our three ladies had their faces all turned toward the speaker, like the weather-cocks in a northeaster, and I thought it best to switch off the talk on to another rail.

"How about the doctors?" I said.

"Theirs is the least learned of the professions, in this country at least. They have not half the general culture of the lawyers, nor a quarter of that of the ministers. I rather think, tho, they are more agreeable to the common run of people than the men with the black coats or the men with green bags. People can swear before 'em if they want to, and they can't very well before ministers. I don't care whether they want to swear or not, they don't want to be on their good behavior. Besides, the minister has a little smack of the sexton about him; he comes when people are *in extremis*, but they don't send for him every time they make a slight moral slip— tell a lie, for instance, or smuggle a silk dress through the custom-house: but they call in the doctor when the child is cutting a tooth or gets a splinter in its finger. So it doesn't mean much to send for him, only a pleasant chat about the news of the day; for putting the baby to rights doesn't take long. Besides, everybody doesn't like to talk about the next world; people are modest in their desires, and find this world as good as they deserve: but everybody loves to talk physic. Everybody loves to hear of strange cases; people are eager to tell the doctor of the wonderful cures they have heard of; they want

35

to know what is the matter with somebody or other who is said to be suffering from "a complication of diseases," and above all to get a hard name, Greek or Latin, for some complaint which sounds altogether too commonplace in plain English. If you will only call a headache a *Cephalalgia*, it acquires dignity at once, and a patient becomes rather proud of it. So I think doctors are generally welcome in most companies."

II

OF THE GENIUS OF EMERSON[2]

EMERSON'S was an Asiatic mind, drawing its sustenance partly from the hard soil of our New England, partly, too, from the air that has known Himalaya and the Ganges. So imprest with this character of his mind was Mr. Burlingame,[3] as I saw him, after his return from his mission, that he said to me, in a freshet of hyperbole, which was the overflow of a channel with a thread of truth running in it, "There are twenty thousand Ralph Waldo Emersons in China."

What could we do with this unexpected, unprovided for, unclassified, half-unwelcome newcomer, who had been for a while potted, as it

[2] From an address before the Massachusetts Historical Society in 1862. Published by Houghton, Mifflin Company.

[3] Anson Burlingame, famous in his time for treaties negotiated between China and the United States, England, Denmark, Sweden, Holland, and Prussia. His son, E. L. Burlingame, has long been the editor of *Scribner's Magazine*.

were, in our Unitarian cold green-house, but had taken to growing so fast that he was lifting off its glass roof and letting in the hailstorms? Here was a protest that outflanked the extreme left of liberalism, yet so calm and serene that its radicalism had the accents of the gospel of peace. Here was an iconoclast without a hammer, who took down our idols from their pedestals so tenderly that it seemed like an act of worship.

The scribes and pharisees made light of his oracular sayings. The lawyers could not find the witnesses to subpœna and the documents to refer to when his case came before them, and turned him over to their wives and daughters. The ministers denounced his heresies, and handled his writings as if they were packages of dynamite, and the grandmothers were as much afraid of his new teachings as old Mrs. Piozzi [4] was of geology. We had had revolutionary orators, reformers, martyrs; it was but a few years since Abner Kneeland had been sent to jail for expressing an opinion about the great First Cause; but we had had nothing like this man, with his seraphic voice and countenance, his choice vocabulary, his refined utterance, his gentle courage, which, with a different manner, might have been called audacity, his temperate statement of opinions which threatened to shake the existing order of thought like an earthquake.

His peculiarities of style and of thinking be-

---

[4] Hester Lynch Salisbury, who married first Henry Thrale, the English brewer, and second an Italian musician named Piozzi; but her fame rests on her friendship of twenty years with Doctor Samuel Johnson, of whom she wrote reminiscences, described by Carlyle as "Piozzi's ginger beer."

came fertile parents of mannerisms, which were fair game for ridicule as they appeared in his imitators. For one who talks like Emerson or like Carlyle soon finds himself surrounded by a crowd of walking phonographs, who mechanically reproduce his mental and vocal accents. Emerson was before long talking in the midst of a babbling Simonetta of echoes, and not unnaturally was now and then himself a mark for the small-shot of criticism. He had soon reached that height in the "cold thin atmosphere" of thought where

> "Vainly the fowler's eye
> Might mark his distant flight to do him wrong."

I shall add a few words, of necessity almost epigrammatic, upon his work and character. He dealt with life, and life with him was not merely this particular air-breathing phase of being, but the spiritual existence which included it like a parenthesis between the two infinities. He wanted his daily drafts of oxygen like his neighbors, and was as thoroughly human as the plain people he mentions who had successively owned or thought they owned the house-lot on which he planted his hearthstone. But he was at home no less in the interstellar spaces outside of all the atmospheres. The semi-materialistic idealism of Milton was a gross and clumsy medium compared to the imponderable ether of "The Oversoul" and the unimaginable vacuum of "Brahma." He followed in the shining and daring track of the *Graius homo* of Lucretius:

> "*Vivida vis animi pervicit, et extra*
> *Processit longe flammantia mœnia mundi.*"

It always seemed to me as if he looked at this earth very much as a visitor from another planet would look upon it. He was interested, and to some extent curious about it, but it was not the first spheroid he had been acquainted with, by any means. I have amused myself with comparing his descriptions of natural objects with those of the Angel Raphael in the seventh book of Paradise Lost. Emerson talks of his titmouse as Raphael talks of his emmet. Angels and poets never deal with nature after the manner of those whom we call naturalists.

To judge of him as a thinker, Emerson should have been heard as a lecturer, for his manner was an illustration of his way of thinking. He would lose his place just as his mind would drop its thought and pick up another, twentieth cousin or no relation at all to it. This went so far at times that one could hardly tell whether he was putting together a mosaic of colored fragments, or only turning a kaleidoscope where the pieces tumbled about as they best might. It was as if he had been looking in at a cosmic peep-show, and turning from it at brief intervals to tell us what he saw. But what fragments these colored sentences were, and what pictures they often placed before us, as if we too saw them! Never has this city known such audiences as he gathered; never was such an Olympian entertainment as that which he gave them.

It is very hard to speak of Mr. Emerson's poetry; not to do it injustice, still more to do it justice. It seems to me like the robe of a monarch patched by a New England housewife. The royal tint and stuff are unmistakable, but here and there the gray worsted from the darning-needle crosses and ekes out the Tyrian purple. Few poets who have written so little in verse have dropped so many of those "jewels five words long" which fall from their setting only to be more choicely treasured. *E pluribus unum* is scarcely more familiar to our ears than "He builded better than he knew," and Keats's "thing of beauty" is little better known than Emerson's "beauty is its own excuse for being." One may not like to read Emerson's poetry because it is sometimes careless, almost as if carefully so, tho never undignified even when slipshod; spotted with quaint archaisms and strange expressions that sound like the affectation of negligence, or with plain, homely phrases such as the self-made scholar is always afraid of. But if one likes Emerson's poetry he will be sure to love it; if he loves it, its phrases will cling to him as hardly any others do. It may not be for the multitude, but it finds its place like pollen-dust and penetrates to the consciousness it is to fertilize and bring to flower and fruit.

I have known something of Emerson as a talker, not nearly so much as many others who can speak and write of him. It is unsafe to tell how a great thinker talks, for perhaps, like a city dealer with a village customer, he has not shown his best goods to the innocent reporter of his sayings. However that may be in this case, let me contrast in a single glance the momentary effect in conversation of the two neighbors, Hawthorne and Emerson. Speech seemed like a kind of travail to Hawthorne. One must harpoon him like a cetacean with questions to make him talk at all. Then the words came from him at last, with bashful manifestations, like those of a young girl, almost—words that gasped themselves forth, seeming to leave a great deal more behind them than they told, and died out discontented with themselves, like the monologue of thunder in the sky, which always goes off mumbling and grumbling as if it had not said half it wanted to, and ought to say. . . .

To sum up briefly what would, as it seems to me, be the text to be unfolded in his biography, he was a man of excellent common sense, with a genius so uncommon that he seemed like an exotic transplanted from some angelic nursery. His character was so blameless, so beautiful, that it was rather a standard to judge others by than to find a place for on the scale of comparison. Looking at life with the profoundest sense of its infinite significance, he was yet a cheerful optimist, almost too hopeful, peeping into every cradle to see if it did not hold a babe with the halo of a new Messiah about it. He enriched the treasure-house of literature, but, what was far more, he enlarged the boundaries of thought for the few that followed him, and the many who never knew, and do not know to-day, what hand it was which took down their prison walls. He was a preacher who taught that the religion of humanity included both those of Palestine, nor those alone, and taught it with such consecrated lips that the narrowest bigot was ashamed to pray for him, as from a footstool nearer to the throne. "Hitch your wagon to a star": this was his version of the divine lesson taught by that holy George Herbert whose words he

loved. Give him whatever place belongs to him
in our literature, in the literature of our language, of the world, but remember this: the end
and aim of his being was to make truth lovely
and manhood valorous, and to bring our daily
life nearer and nearer to the eternal, immortal,
invisible.

III

THE HOUSE IN WHICH THE PROFESSOR LIVED [5]

"THIS is the shortest way," she said, as we
came to a corner.

"Then we won't take it," said I. The schoolmistress laughed a little, and said she was ten
minutes early, so she could go around.

We walked around Mr. Paddock's row of English elms. The gray squirrels were out looking
for their breakfasts, and one of them came toward us in light, soft, intermittent leaps, until
he was close to the rail of the burial ground.
He was on a grave with a broad blue slate-stone
at its head, and a shrub growing on it. The stone
said this was the grave of a young man who
was the son of an honorable gentleman, and who
died a hundred years ago and more. Oh, yes,
died—with a small triangular mark in one breast,
and another smaller opposite, in his back, where
another young man's rapier had slid through

[5] From Part X of "The Autocrat of the Breakfast Table."
Published by Houghton, Mifflin Company.

his body; and so he lay down out there on the
Common, and was found cold the next morning,
with the night dews and the death dews mingled
on his forehead.

"Let us have one look at poor Benjamin's
grave," said I. "His bones lie where his body
was laid so long ago, and where the stone says
they lie—which is more than can be said of most
of the tenants of this and several other burial
grounds. . . .

"Stop before we turn away, and breathe a
woman's sigh over poor Benjamin's dust. Love
killed him, I think. Twenty years old, and out
there fighting another young fellow on the common, in the cool of that old July evening; yes,
there must have been love at the bottom of it."

The schoolmistress dropt a rosebud she had in
her hand through the rails, upon the grave of
Benjamin Woolbridge. That was all her comment upon what I told her. "How women love
Love!" said I; but she did not speak.

We came opposite the head of a place or court
running eastward from the main street. "Look
down there," I said; "my friend, the Professor,
lived in that house, at the left hand, next the
further corner, for years and years. He died
out of it, the other day." "Died?" said the
schoolmistress. "Certainly," said I. "We die
out of houses, just as we die out of our bodies.
A commercial smash kills a hundred men's homes
for them, as a railroad crash kills their mortal
frames and drives out the immortal tenants.
Men sicken of houses until at last they quit
them, as the soul leaves its body when it is tired
of its infirmities. The body has been called 'the

house we live in'; the house is quite as much the body we live in. Shall I tell you some things the Professor said the other day?" "Do!" said the schoolmistress.

" 'A man's body,' said the Professor, 'is whatever is occupied by his will and his sensibility. The small room down there, where I wrote those papers you remember reading, was much more a part of my body than a paralytic's senseless and motionless arm or leg is of his.

" 'The soul of a man has a series of concentric envelopes around it, like the core of an onion, or the innermost of a nest of boxes. First, he has his natural garment of flesh and blood. Then his artificial integuments, with their true skin of solid stuffs, their cuticle of lighter tissues, and their variously tinted pigments. Third, his domicile, be it a single chamber or a stately mansion. And then, the whole visible world, in which Time buttons him up as in a loose outside wrapper.

" 'You shall observe,' the Professor said, for like Mr. John Hunter and other great men, he brings in that 'shall' with great effect sometimes, 'you shall observe that a man's clothing or series of envelopes after a certain time mold themselves upon his individual nature. We know this of our hats, and are always reminded of it when we happen to put them on wrong side foremost. We soon find that the beaver is a hollow cast of the skull, with all its irregular bumps and depressions. Just so all that clothes a man, even to the blue sky which caps his head—a little loosely—shapes itself to fit each particular being beneath it. Farmers, sailors, astronomers, poets, lovers, condemned criminals, all find it different, according to the eyes with which they severally look.

" 'But our houses shape themselves palpably on our inner and outer natures. See a householder breaking up and you will be sure of it. There is a shellfish which builds all manner of smaller shells into the walls of its own. A house is never a home until we have crusted it with the spoils of a hundred lives besides those of our own past. See what these are, and you can tell what the occupant is.

" 'I had no idea,' said the Professor, 'until I pulled up my domestic establishment the other day, what an enormous quantity of roots I had been making the years I was planted there. Why, there wasn't a nook or a corner that some fiber had not worked its way into; and when I gave the last wrench, each of them seemed to shriek like a mandrake, as it broke its hold and came away.

" 'There is nothing that happens, you know, which must not inevitably, and which does not actually, photograph itself in every conceivable aspect and in all dimensions. The infinite galleries of the Past await but one brief process, and all their pictures will be called out and fixt forever. We had a curious illustration of the great fact on a very humble scale. When a certain bookcase, long standing in one place, for which it was built, was removed, there was the exact image on the wall of the whole, and of many of its portions. But in the midst of this picture was another—the precise outline of a map which hung on the wall before the bookcase was built. We had all forgotten everything about the map until we saw its photograph on the wall. Then we remembered it, as some day or other we may remember a sin which has been built over and covered up, when this lower universe is pulled away from the wall of Infinity, where the wrongdoing stands, self-recorded.'

"The Professor lived in that house a long time—not twenty years, but pretty near it. When he entered that door, two shadows glided over the threshold; five lingered in the doorway when he passed through it for the last time—and one of the shadows was claimed by its owner to be longer than his own. What changes he saw in that quiet place! Death rained through every roof but his; children came into life, grew to maturity; wedded, faded away, threw themselves away; the whole drama of life was played in that stock company's theater of a dozen houses, one of which was his, and no deep sorrow or severe calamity ever entered his dwelling. 'Peace be to those walls forever,' the Professor said, for the many pleasant years he has passed within them.

"The Professor has a friend, now living at a distance, who has been with him in many of his changes of place, and who follows him in imagination with tender interest wherever he goes. In that little court, where he lived in gay loneliness so long—in his autumnal sojourn by the Connecticut, where it comes loitering down from its mountain fastnesses like a great lord, swallowing up the small proprietary rivulets very quietly as it goes, until it gets proud and swollen and wantons in huge luxurious oxbows about the fair Northampton meadows, and at last overflows

the oldest inhabitant's memory in profligate
freshets at Hartford and all along its lower
shores—up in that caravansary on the banks of
the stream where Ledyard launched his log canoe,
and the jovial old Colonel used to lead the com-
mencement processions — where blue Ascutney
looked down from the far distance, and the hills
of Beulah, as the Professor always called them,
rolled up the opposite horizon in soft climbing
masses, so suggestive of the Pilgrim's Heaven-
ward Path that he used to look through his old
'Dollond' to see if the Shining Ones were not
within range of sight—sweet visions, sweetest in
those Sunday walks that carried them by the
peaceful common, through the solemn village
lying in cataleptic stillness under the shadows
of the rod of Moses, to the terminus of their
harmless stroll—the 'patulous fage,' in the Professor's classic dialect—the spreading beech, in
more familiar phrase—[stop and breathe here
a moment, for the sentence is not done yet, and
we have another long journey before us.]

"—and again once more up among those other
hills that shut in the amber-flowing Housatonic—
dark stream, but clear, like the lucid orbs that
shine beneath the lids of auburn-haired, sherry-
wine-eyed demiblondes—in the home overlooking
the winding stream and the smooth, flat meadow;
looked down upon by wild hills, where the tracks
of bears and catamounts may yet sometimes be
seen upon the winter snow; facing the twin
summits which rise in the far North, the highest
waves of the great land storm in this billowy
region—suggestive to mad fancies of the breasts
of a half-buried Titaness, stretched out by a

stray thunderbolt, and hastily hidden away beneath the leaves of the forest—in that home where seven blest summers were passed, which stand in memory like the seven golden candlesticks in the beatific vision of the holy dreamer—

"—in that modest dwelling we were just looking at, not glorious, yet not unlovely in the youth of its drab and mahogany—full of great and little boys' playthings from top to bottom—in all these summer or winter nests he was always at home and always welcome.

"This long articulated sigh of reminiscences—this calenture which shows me the maple-shadowed plains of Berkshire and the mountain-circled green of Grafton beneath the salt waves that come feeling their way along the wall at my feet, restless and soft-touching as blind men's busy fingers—is for that friend of mine who looks into the waters of the Patapsco and sees beneath them the same visions that paint themselves for me in the green depths of the Charles."

Did I talk all this off to the schoolmistress? Why, no—of course not. I have been talking with you, the reader, for the last ten minutes. You don't think I should expect any woman to listen to such a sentence as that long one, without giving her a chance to put in a word?

What did I say to the schoolmistress? Permit me one moment. I don't doubt your delicacy and good-breeding; but in this particular case, as I was allowed the privilege of walking alone with a very interesting young woman, you must allow me to remark, in the classic version of a familiar phrase, used by our Master Benjamin Franklin, it is *nullum tui negotii.*

When the schoolmistress and I reached the schoolroom door, the damask roses I spoke of were so much heightened in color by exercise that I felt sure it would be useful to her to take a stroll like this every morning, and made up my mind I would ask her to let me join her again.

IV

OF WOMEN WHO PUT ON AIRS⁶

I CAN'T say just how many walks she (the schoolmistress) and I had taken together before this one. I found the effect of going out every morning was decidedly favorable on her health. Two pleasing dimples, the places for which were just marked when she came, played, shadowy, in her freshening cheeks when she smiled and nod-ded good-morning to me from the schoolhouse steps.

I am afraid I did the greater part of the talk-ing. At any rate, if I should try to report all that I said during the first half-dozen walks we took together, I fear that I might receive a gentle hint from my friends the publishers that a separate volume, at my own risk and expense, would be the proper method of bringing them before the public.

I would have a woman as true as death. At the first real lie which works from the heart

⁶ From Part XI of "The Autocrat of the Breakfast Table." Published by Houghton, Mifflin Company.

outward she should be tenderly chloroformed into a better world, where she can have an angel for a governess, and feed on strange fruits which will make her all over again, even to her bones and marrow. Whether gifted with the accident of beauty or not, she should have been molded in the rose-red clay of love before the breath of life made a moving mortal of her. Love capacity is a congenital endowment; and I think, after a while, one gets to know the warm-hued natures it belongs to from the pretty pipe-clay counterfeits of it. Proud she may be, in the sense of respecting herself; but pride, in the sense of contemning others less gifted than herself, deserves the two lowest circles of a vulgar woman's Inferno, where the punishments are smallpox and bankruptcy. She who nips off the end of a brittle courtesy, as one breaks the tip of an icicle, to bestow upon those whom she ought cordially and kindly to recognize, proclaims the fact that she comes not merely of low blood, but of bad blood. Consciousness of unquestioned position makes people gracious in proper measure to all; but if a woman puts on airs with her real equals, she has something about herself or her family she is ashamed of, or ought to be. Middle, and more than middle-aged people, who know family histories, generally see through it. An official of standing was rude to me once. "Oh, that is the maternal grandfather," said a wise old friend to me, "he was a boor." Better too few words, from the woman we love, than too many: while she is silent, Nature is working for her; while she talks, she is working for herself. Love is sparingly soluble in the words of men; therefore they speak much of it; but one syllable of woman's speech can dissolve more of it than a man's heart can hold.

Whether I said any or all of these things to the schoolmistress or not—whether I stole them out of Lord Bacon—whether I cribbed them from Balzac—whether I dipt them from the ocean of Tupperian wisdom—or whether I have just found them in my head (laid there by that solemn fowl, Experience, who, according to my observation, cackles oftener than she drops real, live eggs), I can not say. Wise men have said more foolish things—and foolish men, I don't doubt, have said as wise things. Anyhow, the schoolmistress and I had pleasant walks and long talks, all of which I do not feel bound to report.

You are a stranger to me, Ma'am.—I don't doubt you would like to know all I said to the schoolmistress.—I shan't do it; I had rather get the publishers to return the money you have invested in this. Besides, I have forgotten a good deal of it. I shall tell only what I like of what I remember.

MARGARET FULLER

Born in Massachusetts in 1810; lost in a shipwreck off
Fire Island in 1850; edited *The Dial* in 1840-42; literary
critic for the New York *Tribune* in 1844-46; went to Europe
in 1846; married the Marquis d'Ossoli in 1847; in Rome
during the Revolution of 1848-49; published "A Summer
on the Lakes" in 1843, "Woman in the Nineteenth Century"
in 1845, "Papers on Art and Literature" in 1846.

I

HER VISIT TO GEORGE SAND [1]

IT is the custom to go and call on those to
whom you bring letters, and push yourself upon
their notice; thus you must go quite ignorant
whether they are disposed to be cordial. My
name is always murdered by the foreign servants
who announce me. I speak very bad French;
only lately have I had sufficient command of it
to infuse some of my natural spirit in my discourse. This has been a great trial to me, who
am eloquent and free in my own tongue, to be
forced to feel my thoughts struggling in vain
for utterance.

The servant who admitted me was in the picturesque costume of a peasant, and as Madame
Sand afterward told me, her goddaughter, whom
she had brought from her province. She announced me as "Madame Salère," and returned

[1] From a letter to Elizabeth Hoar, written in 1847 and
printed in the "Memoirs."

52

into the anteroom to tell me, "Madame says she does not know you." I began to think I was doomed to rebuff among the crowd who deserve it. However, to make assurance sure, I said, "Ask if she has received a letter from me." As I spoke Madame Sand opened the door, and stood looking at me an instant. Our eyes met.

I never shall forget her look at that moment. The doorway made a frame for her figure; she is large but well formed. She was drest in a robe of dark-violet silk, with a black mantle on her shoulders, her beautiful hair drest with the greatest taste; her whole appearance and attitude, in its simple and ladylike dignity, presented an almost ludicrous contrast to the vulgar caricature idea of George Sand. Her face is a very little like the portraits, but much finer; the upper part of the forehead and eyes are beautiful, the lower strong and masculine, expressive of a hardy temperament and strong passions, but not in the least coarse; the complexion olive, and the air of the whole head Spanish (as, indeed, she was born at Madrid, and is only on one side of French blood).

All these I saw at a glance; but what fixt my attention was the expression of goodness, nobleness, and power that pervaded the whole—the truly human heart and nature that shone in the eyes. As our eyes met, she said, *"C'est vous,"* and held out her hand. I took it, and went into her little study; we sat down a moment; then I said, *"Il me fait de bien de vous voir,"* and I am sure I said it with my whole heart, for it made me very happy to see such a woman, so large and so developed in character, and everything that is good in it so really good. I loved, shall always love her.

She looked away, and said, "*Ah! vous m'avez écrit une lettre charmante.*" This was all the preliminary of our talk, which then went on as if we had always known one another. . . . Her way of talking is just like her writing— lively, picturesque, with an undertone of deep feeling, and the same happiness in striking the nail on the head every now and then with a blow. . . . I heartily enjoyed the sense of so rich, so prolific, so ardent a genius. I liked the woman in her, too, very much; I never liked a woman better. . . . For the rest, she holds her place in the literary and social world of France like a man, and seems full of energy and courage in it. I suppose she has suffered much, but she has also enjoyed and done much.

II

TWO GLIMPSES OF CARLYLE [2]

Of the people I saw in London you will wish me to speak first of the Carlyles. Mr. Carlyle came to see me at once, and appointed an evening to be passed at their house. That first time I was delighted with him. He was in a very sweet humor—full of wit and pathos, without being overbearing or oppressive. I was quite

[2] From a letter to Emerson, written in 1846, and printed in the "Memoirs."

carried away with the rich flow of his discourse; and the hearty, noble earnestness of his personal being brought back the charm which once was upon his writing, before I wearied of it. I admired his Scotch, his way of singing his great full sentences, so that each one was like the stanza of a narrative ballad. He let me talk, now and then, enough to free my lungs and change my position, so that I did not get tired. That evening he talked of the present state of things in England, giving light, witty sketches of the men of the day, fanatics and others, and some sweet, homely stories he told of things he had known of the Scotch peasantry. Of you he spoke with hearty kindness; and he told with beautiful feeling a story of some poor farmer or artizan in the country, who on Sunday lays aside the cark and care of that dirty English world, and sits reading the "Essays" and looking upon the sea. . . .

The second time Mr. Carlyle had a dinner party, at which was a witty, French, flippant sort of a man, named Lewes,[*] author of a "History of Philosophy," and now writing a life of Goethe, a task for which he must be as unfit as irreligion and sparkling shallowness can make him. But he told stories admirably, and was allowed sometimes to interrupt Carlyle a little— of which one was glad, for that night he was in his acrid mood; and tho much more brilliant than on the former evening, grew wearisome to me,

[*] George Henry Lewes, whose relations to George Eliot began after Margaret Fuller's visit. Lewes was not a Frenchman, but of Welsh descent, born in London, and a grandson of Charles Lee Lewes, the actor.

who disclaimed and rejected almost everything he said. . . .

Accustomed to the infinite wit and exuberant richness of his writings, his talk is still an amazement and a splendor scarcely to be faced with steady eyes. He does not converse, only harangues. It is the usual misfortune of such marked men—happily not one invariable or inevitable—that they can not allow other minds room to breathe, and show themselves in their atmosphere, and thus miss the refreshment and instruction which the greatest never cease to need from the experience of the humblest. Carlyle allows no one a chance, but bears down all opposition, not only by his wit and onset of words, resistless in their sharpness as so many bayonets, but by actual physical superiority — raising his voice and rushing on his opponent with a torrent of sound. This is not in the least from unwillingness to allow freedom to others. On the contrary, no man would more enjoy a manly resistance in his thoughts. But it is the impulse of a mind accustomed to follow out its own impulse, as the hawk its prey, and which knows not how to stop in the chase.

Carlyle indeed is arrogant and overbearing; but in his arrogance there is no littleness, no self-love. It is the heroic arrogance of some old Scandinavian conqueror; it is his nature, and the untamable impulse that has given him power to crush the dragons. He sings rather than talks. He pours upon you a kind of satirical, heroical, critical poem, with regular cadences, and generally catching up, near the beginning, some singular epithet which serves as a refrain when his song is full, or with which, as with a knitting-needle, he catches up the stitches, if he has chanced now and then to let fall a row. For the higher kinds of poetry he has no sense, and his talk on that subject is delightfully and gorgeously absurd. He sometimes stops a minute to laugh at it himself, then begins anew with fresh vigor; for all the spirits he is driving before him as Fata Morgana,[*] ugly masks, in fact, if he can but make them turn about; but he laughs that they seem to others such dainty Ariels. His talk, like his books, is full of pictures; his critical strokes masterly. Allow for his point of view, and his survey is admirable. He is a large subject. I can not speak more or wiselier of him now, nor needs it; his works are true, to blame and praise him —the Siegfried of England, great and powerful, if not quite invulnerable, and of a might rather to destroy evil than legislate for good.

[*] Fata (a fairy) Morgana, sister of King Arthur, is a leading figure in the "Morte d'Arthur" and other romances, including Italian.

HORACE GREELEY

Born in New Hampshire in 1811, died in 1872; came to
New York in 1831, where he edited the *Log Cabin* during
the Harrison-Tyler campaign; in 1841 founded *The Tribune;*
member of Congress in 1848-49; prominent as an anti-
slavery leader and supporter of the Union cause; nominated
for president by the Liberal-Republican and Democratic
parties in 1872, but defeated by Gen. Grant; published
"Recollections of a Busy Life" in 1868, and "The American
Conflict" in 1864-66.

I

THE FATALITY OF SELF-SEEKING IN EDITORS AND AUTHORS[1]

It only remains to me to speak more especially
of my own vocation—the editor's—which bears
much the same relation to the author's that the
bellows-blower's bears to the organist's, the play-
er's to the dramatist's, Julian or Liszt to Weber
or Beethoven. The editor, from the absolute
necessity of the case, can not speak deliberately;
he must write to-day of to-day's incidents and
aspects, tho these may be completely overlaid
and transformed by the incidents and aspects
of to-morrow. He must write and strive in the
full consciousness that whatever honor or distinction he may acquire must perish with the
generation that bestowed them—with the thun-
ders of applause that greeted Kemble or Jenny

[1] Printed with the "Miscellanies" in the "Recollections of
a Busy Life."

58

Lind, with the ruffianism that expelled Macready,
or the cheerful laugh that erewhile rewarded the
sallies of Burton or Placide.[9]

No other public teacher lives so wholly in the
present as the editor; and the noblest affirma-
tions of unpopular truth—the most self-sac-
rificing defiance of a base and selfish public sentiment that regards only the most sordid ends,
and values every utterance solely as it tends
to preserve quiet and contentment, while the
dollars fall jingling into the merchant's drawer,
the land-jobber's vault, and the miser's bag—can
but be noted in their day, and with their day
forgotten. It is his cue to utter silken and
smooth sayings—to condemn vice so as not to
interfere with the pleasures or alarm the conscience of the vicious—to praise and champion
liberty so as not to give annoyance or offense
to slavery, and to commend and glorify labor
without attempting to expose or repress any of
the gainful contrivances by which labor is plundered and degraded. Thus sidling dextrously between somewhere and nowhere, the able editor
of the nineteenth century may glide through life
respectable and in good ease, and lie down to
his long rest with the non-achievements of his
life emblazoned on the very whitest marble, sur-
mounting and glorifying his dust.

There is a different and sterner path—I know
not whether there be any now qualified to tread
it—I am not sure that even one has ever followed
it implicitly, in view of the certain meagerness

---

[9] Henry Placide, an American actor born in Charleston,
who excelled in the parts of Sir Peter Teazle and Sir An-
thony Absolute.

of its temporal rewards and the haste wherewith any fame acquired in a sphere so thoroughly ephemeral as the editor's must be shrouded by the dark waters of oblivion. This path demands an ear ever open to the plaints of the wronged and the suffering, tho they can never repay advocacy, and those who mainly support newspapers will be annoyed and often exposed by it; a heart as sensitive to oppression and degradation in the next street as if they were practised in Brazil or Japan; a pen as ready to expose and reprove the crimes whereby wealth is amassed and luxury enjoyed in our own country at this hour as if they had only been committed by Turks or pagans in Asia some centuries ago.

Such an editor, could one be found or trained, need not expect to lead an easy, indolent, or wholly joyous life—to be blest by archbishops or followed by the approving shouts of ascendent majorities; but he might find some recompense for their loss in the calm verdict of an approving conscience; and the tears of the despised and the friendless, preserved from utter despair by his efforts and remonstrances, might freshen for a season the daisies that bloomed above his grave.

Literature is a noble calling, but only when the call obeyed by the aspirant issues from a world to be enlightened and blest, not from a void stomach clamoring to be gratified and filled. Authorship is a royal priesthood; but wo to him who rashly lays unhallowed hands on the ark or the altar, professing a zeal for the welfare of the race only that he may secure the confidence and sympathies of others, and use them for his own selfish ends! If a man have no heroism in his soul—no animating purpose beyond living easily and faring sumptuously—I can imagine no greater mistake on his part than that of resorting to authorship as a vocation. That such a one may achieve what he regards as success I do not deny; but, if so, he does it at greater risk and by greater exertion than would have been required to win it in any other pursuit. No; it can not be wise in a selfish, or sordid, or sensual man to devote himself to literature; the fearful self-exposure incident to this way of life—the dire necessity which constrains the author to stamp his own essential portrait on every volume of his works, no matter how carefully he may fancy he has erased, or how artfully he may suppose he has concealed it—this should repel from the vestibule of the temple of fame the foot of every profane or mocking worshiper.

But if you are sure that your impulse is not personal nor sinister, but a desire to serve and ennoble your race, rather than to dazzle and be served by it; that you are ready joyfully to "scorn delights, and live laborious days," so that thereby the well-being of mankind may be promoted—then I pray you not to believe that the world is too wise to need further enlightenment, nor that it would be impossible for one so humble as yourself to say aught whereby error may be dispelled or good be diffused. Sell not your integrity; barter not your independence; beg of no man the privilege of earning a livelihood by authorship; since that is to degrade your faculty, and very probably to corrupt it; but seeing through your own clear eyes, and uttering the impulses of your own honest heart, speak or write as truth and love shall dictate, asking no material recompense, but living by the labor of your hands, until recompense shall be voluntarily tendered to secure your service, and you may frankly accept it without a compromise of your integrity or a peril to your freedom. Soldier in the long warfare for man's rescue from darkness and evil, choose not your place on the battle-field, but joyfully accept that assigned you; asking not whether there be higher or lower, but only whether it is here that you can most surely do your proper work, and meet your full share of the responsibility and the danger.

Believe not that the heroic age is no more; since to that age is only requisite the heroic purpose and the heroic soul. So long as ignorance and evil shall exist so long there will be work for the devoted, and so long will there be room in the ranks of those who, defying obloquy, misapprehension, bigotry, and interested craft, struggle and dare for the redemption of the world. "Of making many books there is no end," tho there is happily a speedy end of most books after they are made; but he who by voice or pen strikes his best blow at the impostures and vices whereby our race is debased and paralyzed may close his eyes in death, consoled and cheered by the reflection that he has done what he could for the emancipation and elevation of his kind.

JOHN LOTHROP MOTLEY

Born in 1814, died in 1877; graduated from Harvard in 1831; studied at Göttingen and Berlin; returned to America in 1834 and admitted to the bar, but soon took up the study of history; United States minister to Austria in 1861-68, and to Great Britain in 1869-70; published his "Rise of the Dutch Republic" in 1856, "History of the United Netherlands" in 1860-67, and "John of Barneveld" in 1874.

I

CHARLES V AND PHILIP II IN BRUSSELS[1]
(1555)

THE Emperor, like many potentates before and since, was fond of great political spectacles. He knew their influence upon the masses of mankind. Altho plain even to shabbiness in his own costume, and usually attired in black, no one ever understood better than he how to arrange such exhibitions in a striking and artistic style. We have seen the theatrical and imposing manner in which he quelled the insurrection at Ghent, and nearly crusht the life forever out of that vigorous and turbulent little commonwealth. The closing scene of his long and energetic reign he had now arranged with profound study, and with an accurate knowledge of the manner in which the requisite effects were to be produced. The

---

[1] From Chapter I of the "The Rise of the Dutch Republic." Published by Harper & Brothers. After his abdication Charles V retired to a monastery, where he died three years later.

termination of his own career, the opening of his beloved Philip's, were to be dramatized in a manner worthy the august characters of the actors, and the importance of the great stage where they played their parts. The eyes of the whole world were directed upon that day toward Brussels; for an imperial abdication was an event which had not, in the sixteenth century, been staled by custom.

The gay capital of Brabant—of that province which rejoiced in the liberal constitution known by the cheerful title of the "joyful entrance"—was worthy to be the scene of the imposing show. Brussels had been a city for more than five centuries, and at that day numbered about one hundred thousand inhabitants. Its walls, six miles in circumference, were already two hundred years old. Unlike most Netherland cities, lying usually upon extensive plains, it was built along the sides of an abrupt promontory. A wide expanse of living verdure—cultivated gardens, shady groves, fertile cornfields—flowed round it like a sea. The foot of the town was washed by the little river Senne, while the irregular but picturesque streets rose up the steep sides of the hill like the semicircles and stairways of an amphitheater. Nearly in the heart of the place rose the audacious and exquisitely embroidered tower of the town-house, three hundred and sixty-six feet in height; a miracle of needlework in stone, rivaling in its intricate carving the cobweb tracery of that lace which has for centuries been synonymous with the city, and rearing itself above a façade of profusely decorated and brocaded architecture. The crest of the elevation was crowned by the towers of the old ducal palace of Brabant, with its extensive and thickly wooded park on the left, and by the stately mansions of Orange, Egmont, Aremberg, Culemburg, and other Flemish grandees, on the right. . . .

The palace where the states-general were upon this occasion convened had been the residence of the dukes of Brabant since the days of John the Second, who had built it about the year 1300. It was a spacious and convenient building, but not distinguished for the beauty of its architecture. In front was a large open square, enclosed by an iron railing; in the rear an extensive and beautiful park, filled with forest trees, and containing gardens and labyrinths, fish-ponds and game preserves, fountains and promenades, race-courses and archery grounds. The main entrance to this edifice opened upon a spacious hall, connected with a beautiful and symmetrical chapel. The hall was celebrated for its size, harmonious proportions, and the richness of its decorations. It was the place where the chapters of the famous order of the Golden Fleece were held. Its walls were hung with a magnificent tapestry of Arras, representing the life and achievements of Gideon the Midianite, and giving particular prominence to the miracle of the "fleece of wool," vouchsafed to that renowned champion, the great patron of the Knights of the Fleece.

On the present occasion there were various additional embellishments of flowers and votive garlands. At the western end a spacious platform or stage, with six or seven steps, had been constructed, below which was a range of benches for the deputies of the seventeen provinces. Upon the stage itself there were rows of seats, covered with tapestry, upon the right hand and upon the left. These were respectively to accommodate the knights of the order and the guests of high distinction. In the rear of these were other benches for the members of the three great councils. In the center of the stage was a splendid canopy, decorated with the arms of Burgundy, beneath which were placed three gilded armchairs. All the seats upon the platform were vacant; but the benches below, assigned to the deputies of the provinces, were already filled. Numerous representatives from all the States but two—Gelderland and Overyssel—had already taken their places. Grave magistrates in chain and gown, and executive officers in the splendid civic uniforms for which the Netherlands were celebrated, already filled every seat within the space allotted. The remainder of the hall was crowded with the more favored portion of the multitude, which had been fortunate enough to procure admission to the exhibition. The archers and halbardiers of the body-guard kept watch at all the doors. The theater was filled, the audience was eager with expectation, the actors were yet to arrive.

As the clock struck three, the hero of the scene appeared. Cæsar, as he was always designated in the classic language of the day, entered, leaning on the shoulder of William of Orange. They came from the chapel, and were immediately followed by Philip the Second and Queen Mary of Hungary. The Archduke Maximilian, the

Duke of Savoy, and other great personages came afterward, accompanied by a glittering throng of warriors, councilors, governors, and Knights of the Fleece.

Many individuals of existing or future historic celebrity in the Netherlands, whose names are so familiar to the student of the epoch, seemed to have been grouped, as if by premeditated design, upon this imposing platform, where the curtain was to fall forever upon the mightiest emperor since Charlemagne, and where the opening scene of the long and tremendous tragedy of Philip's reign was to be simultaneously enacted. There was the bishop of Arras, soon to be known throughout Christendom by the more celebrated title of Cardinal Granvelle—the serene and smiling priest, whose subtle influence over the destinies of so many individuals then present, and over the fortunes of the whole land, was to be so extensive and so deadly. There was that flower of Flemish chivalry, the lineal descendant of ancient Frisian kings, already distinguished for his bravery in many fields, but not having yet won those two remarkable victories which were soon to make the name of Egmont like the sound of a trumpet throughout the whole country. Tall, magnificent in costume, with dark flowing hair, soft brown eye, smooth cheek, a slight mustache, and features of almost feminine delicacy—such was the gallant and ill-fated Lamoral Egmont. The Count of Hoorne,[2] too, with bold, sullen face, and fan-shaped beard—a brave, honest, discontented, quarrelsome, unpopular

[2] See Prescott's account of the execution of Egmont and Hoorne, in Volume IX of this collection.

man; those other twins in doom, the Marquis Berghen and the Lord of Montigny; the Baron Berlaymont, brave, intensely loyal, insatiably greedy for office and wages, but who at least never served but one party; the Duke of Arschot, who was to serve all, essay to rule all, and to betray all—a splendid seignior, magnificent in cramoisy velvet, but a poor creature, who traced his pedigree from Adam according to the family monumental inscriptions at Louvain, but who was better known as grandnephew of the Emperor's famous tutor Chièvres; the bold, debauched Brederode, with handsome, reckless face and turbulent demeanor; the infamous Noircarmes, whose name was to be covered with eternal execration for aping toward his own compatriots and kindred as much of Alva's atrocities and avarice as he was permitted to exercise; the distinguished soldiers Meghen and Aremberg—these, with many others whose deeds of arms were to become celebrated throughout Europe, were all conspicuous in the brilliant crowd. There, too, was that learned Frisian, President Viglius, crafty, plausible, adroit, eloquent—a small, brisk man, with long yellow hair, glittering green eyes, round, tumid, rosy cheeks, and flowing beard. Foremost among the Spanish grandees, and close to Philip, stood the famous favorite, Ruy Gomez, or, as he was familiarly called, "*Re y Gomez*" (King and Gomez)—a man of meridional aspect, with coal-black hair and beard, gleaming eyes, a face pallid with intense application, and slender but handsome figure; while in immediate attendance upon the Emperor was the immortal Prince of Orange.

Such were a few only of the most prominent in that gay throng, whose fortunes in part it will be our humble duty to narrate; how many of them passing through all this glitter to a dark and mysterious gloom! some to perish on public scaffolds, some by midnight assassination; others, more fortunate, to fall on the battle-field; nearly all, sooner or later, to be laid in bloody graves!

All the company present had risen to their feet as the Emperor entered. By his command, all immediately after resumed their places. The benches at either end of the platform were accordingly filled with the royal and princely personages invited—with the Fleece Knights, wearing the insignia of their order, with the members of the three great councils, and with the governors. The Emperor, the King, and the Queen of Hungary were left conspicuous in the center of the scene. As the whole object of the ceremony was to present an impressive exhibition, it is worth our while to examine minutely the appearance of the two principal characters.

Charles the Fifth was then fifty-five years and eight months old; but he was already decrepit with premature old age. He was of about the middle height; and had been athletic and well proportioned. Broad in the shoulders, deep in the chest, thin in the flank, very muscular in the arms and legs, he had been able to match himself with all competitors in the tourney and the ring, and to vanquish the bull with his own hand in the favorite national amusement of Spain. He had been able in the field to do the duty of captain and soldier, to endure fatigue and exposure, and every privation except fasting.

These personal advantages were now departed. Crippled in hands, knees, and legs, he supported himself with difficulty upon a crutch, with the aid of an attendant's shoulder. In face he had always been extremely ugly, and time had certainly not improved his physiognomy. His hair, once of a light color, was now white with age, close-clipt and bristling; his beard was gray, coarse, and shaggy. His forehead was spacious and commanding; the eye was dark-blue, with an expression both majestic and benignant. His nose was aquiline but crooked. The lower part of his face was famous for its deformity. The under lip, a Burgundian inheritance, as faithfully transmitted as the duchy and county, was heavy and hanging; the lower jaw protruding so far beyond the upper that it was impossible for him to bring together the few fragments of teeth which still remained, or to speak a whole sentence in an intelligible voice. Eating and talking, occupations to which he was always much addicted, were becoming daily more arduous in consequence of this original defect; which now seemed hardly human, but rather an original deformity.

So much for the father. The son, Philip the Second, was a small, meager man, much below the middle height, with thin legs, a narrow chest, and the shrinking, timid air of a habitual invalid. He seemed so little upon his first visit to his aunts, the Queens Eleanor and Mary, accustomed to look upon proper men in Flanders and Germany, that he was fain to win their favor by making certain attempts in the tournament, in which his success was sufficiently problematical.

"His body," says his profest panegyrist, "was but a human cage, in which, however brief and narrow, dwelt a soul to whose flight the immeasurable expanse of heaven was too contracted." The same wholesale admirer adds that "his aspect was so reverend that rustics who met him alone in the wood, without knowing him, bowed down with instinctive veneration." In face he was the living image of his father; having the same broad forehead and blue eye, with the same aquiline, but better proportioned, nose. In the lower part of the countenance the remarkable Burgundian deformity was likewise reproduced: he had the same heavy, hanging lip, with a vast mouth, and monstrously protruding lower jaw. His complexion was fair, his hair light and thin, his beard yellow, short, and pointed. He had the aspect of a Fleming, but the loftiness of a Spaniard. His demeanor in public was still, silent, almost sepulchral. He looked habitually on the ground when he conversed, was chary of speech, embarrassed and even suffering in manner. This was ascribed partly to a natural haughtiness, which he had occasionally endeavored to overcome, and partly to habitual pains in the stomach, occasioned by his inordinate fondness for pastry.

Such was the personal appearance of the man who was about to receive into his single hand the destinies of half the world; whose single will was, for the future, to shape the fortunes of every individual then present, of many millions more in Europe, America, and at the ends of the earth, and of countless millions yet unborn. . . .

The Emperor then rose to his feet. Leaning on his crutch, he beckoned from his seat the personage upon whose arm he had leaned as he entered the hall. A tall, handsome youth of twenty-two came forward: a man whose name from that time forward, and as long as history shall endure, has been and will be more familiar than any other in the mouths of Netherlanders. At that day he had rather a southern than a German or Flemish appearance. He had a Spanish cast of features, dark, well chiseled, and symmetrical. His head was small and well placed upon his shoulders. His hair was dark brown, as were also his mustache and peaked beard. His forehead was lofty, spacious, and already prematurely engraved with the anxious lines of thought. His eyes were full, brown, well opened, and expressive of profound reflection. He was drest in the magnificent apparel for which the Netherlanders were celebrated above all other nations, and which the ceremony rendered necessary. His presence being considered indispensable at this great ceremony, he had been summoned but recently from the camp on the frontier, where, notwithstanding his youth, the Emperor had appointed him to command his army in chief against such antagonists as Admiral Coligny and the Duc de Nevers.

Thus supported upon his crutch and upon the shoulder of William of Orange, the Emperor proceeded to address the States, by the aid of a closely written brief which he held in his hand. He reviewed rapidly the progress of events from his seventeenth year up to that day. Turning to Philip, he observed that for a dying father to bequeath so magnificent an empire to his son was a deed worthy of gratitude; but that when the father thus descended to the grave before his time, and by an anticipated and living burial sought to provide for the welfare of his realms and the grandeur of his son, the benefit thus conferred was surely far greater. He added that the debt would be paid to him and with usury, should Philip conduct himself in his administration of the province with a wise and affectionate regard to their true interests. . . .

Sobs were heard throughout every portion of the hall, and tears poured profusely from every eye. The Fleece Knights on the platform and the burghers in the background were all melted with the same emotion. As for the Emperor himself, he sank almost fainting upon his chair as he concluded his address. An ashy paleness overspread his countenance, and he wept like a child. Even the icy Philip was almost softened, as he rose to perform his part in the ceremony. Dropping upon his knees before his father's feet, he reverently kissed his hand. Charles placed his hands solemnly upon his son's head, made the sign of the cross, and blest him in the name of the Holy Trinity. Then raising him in his arms he tenderly embraced him, saying, as he did so, to the great potentates around him, that he felt a sincere compassion for the son on whose shoulders so heavy a weight had just devolved, and which only a lifelong labor would enable him to support. . . .

The orations and replies having now been brought to a close, the ceremony was terminated. The Emperor, leaning on the shoulders of the Prince of Orange and of the Count de Buren, slowly left the hall, followed by Philip, the Queen of Hungary, and the whole court; all in the same order in which they had entered, and by the same passage into the chapel.

II

THE ARRIVAL OF THE SPANISH ARMADA [3]
(1588)

ALMOST at that very instant intelligence had been brought from the court to the Lord Admiral at Plymouth that the Armada, dispersed and shattered by the gales of June, was not likely to make its appearance that year; and orders had consequently been given to disarm the four largest ships and send them into dock. Even Walsingham had participated in this strange delusion.

Before Howard [4] had time to act upon this ill-timed suggestion—even had he been disposed to do so—he received authentic intelligence that the great fleet was off the Lizard. Neither he nor Francis Drake were the men to lose time in such an emergency; and before that Friday night was spent, sixty of the best English ships had been warped out of Plymouth harbor.

On Saturday, 30th July, the wind was very

[3] From Chapter XIX of the "History of the United Netherlands." Published by Harper & Brothers. See Hume's account of the arrival of the Armada in Volume IV, page 113, of this collection.

[4] Lord Howard of Effingham, commander of the English fleet.

light at southwest, with a mist and drizzling
rain; but by three in the afternoon the two fleets
could descry and count each other through the
haze.

By nine o'clock, 31st July, about two miles
from Looe on the Cornish coast, the fleets had
their first meeting. There were one hundred and
thirty-six sail of the Spaniards, of which ninety
were large ships; and sixty-seven of the English.
It was a solemn moment. The long-expected
Armada presented a pompous, almost a theatrical
appearance. The ships seemed arranged for a
pageant, in honor of a victory already won. Disposed in form of a crescent, the horns of which
were seven miles asunder, those gilded, towered,
floating castles, with their gaudy standards and
their martial music, moved slowly along the channel, with an air of indolent pomp. Their captain-
general, the golden duke, stood in his private
shot-proof fortress, on the deck of his great
galleon the *St. Martin*, surrounded by generals
of infantry and colonels of cavalry, who knew
as little as he did himself of naval matters.

The English vessels, on the other hand—with
a few exceptions light, swift, and easily handled—could sail round and round those unwieldy
galleons, hulks, and galleys rowed by fettered
slave gangs. The superior seamanship of free
Englishmen commanded by such experienced
captains as Drake, Frobisher,[5] and Hawkins[6]

---

[5] Sir Martin Frobisher, who in 1576 commanded an expedition in search of the Northwest Passage, and discovered
the bay since called after him.

[6] Sir John Hawkins at this time was a rear-admiral. He
was knighted after the defeat of the Armada.

—from infancy at home on blue water—was
manifest in the very first encounter. They obtained the weather-gage at once, and cannonaded
the enemy at intervals with considerable effect;
easily escaping at will out of range of the slug-
gish Armada, which was incapable of bearing sail
in pursuit, altho provided with an armament
which could sink all its enemies at close quarters.
"We had some small fight with them that Sunday
afternoon," said Hawkins.

Medina Sidonia [7] hoisted the royal standard at
the fore; and the whole fleet did its utmost,
which was little, to offer general battle. It was
in vain. The English, following at the heels of
the enemy, refused all such invitations, and attacked only the rear-guard of the Armada, where
Recalde commanded. That admiral, steadily
maintaining his post, faced his nimble antagonists, who continued to tease, to maltreat, and
to elude him, while the rest of the fleet proceeded
slowly up the Channel closely followed by the
enemy. And thus the running fight continued
along the coast, in full view of Plymouth, whence
boats with reenforcements and volunteers were
perpetually arriving to the English ships, until
the battle had drifted quite out of reach of the
town.

Already in this first "small fight" the Spaniards had learned a lesson, and might even enter-
tain a doubt of their invincibility. But before
the sun set there were more serious disasters.
Much powder and shot had been expended by
the Spaniard to very little purpose, and so a

[7] The Duke of Medina Sidonia, who commanded the
Armada.

master-gunner on board Admiral Oquendo's flag-ship was reprimanded for careless ball-practise. The gunner, who was a Fleming, enraged with his captain, laid a train to the powder-magazine, fired it, and threw himself into the sea. Two decks blew up. The great castle at the stern rose into clouds, carrying with it the paymaster-general of the fleet, a large portion of treasure, and nearly two hundred men. The ship was a wreck, but it was possible to save the rest of the crew. So Medina Sidonia sent light vessels to remove them, and wore with his flag-ship to defend Oquendo, who had already been fastened upon by his English pursuers. But the Span-iards, not being so light in hand as their enemies, involved themselves in much embarrassment by their maneuver, and there was much falling foul of each other, entanglement of rigging, and car-rying away of yards. Oquendo's men, however, were ultimately saved and taken to other ships.

Meantime Don Pedro de Valdez, commander of the Andalusian squadron, having got his gal-leon into collision with two or three Spanish ships successively, had at last carried away his fore-mast close to the deck, and the wreck had fallen against his main-mast. He lay crippled and help-less, the Armada was slowly deserting him, night was coming on, the sea was running high, and the English, ever hovering near, were ready to grapple with him. In vain did Don Pedro fire signals of distress. The captain-general—even as tho the unlucky galleon had not been con-nected with the Catholic fleet—calmly fired a gun to collect his scattered ships, and abandoned Val-dez to his fate. "He left me comfortless in sight of the whole fleet," said poor Pedro; "and greater inhumanity and unthankfulness I think was never heard of among men."

Yet the Spaniard comported himself most gallantly. Frobisher, in the largest ship of the English fleet, the *Triumph*, of eleven hundred tons, and Hawkins in the *Victory*, of eight hundred, cannonaded him at a distance, but night coming on, he was able to resist; and it was not till the following morning that he surrendered to the *Revenge*.

Drake then received the gallant prisoner on board his flagship—much to the disgust and indignation of Frobisher and Hawkins, thus disappointed of their prize and ransom money — treated him with much courtesy, and gave his word of honor that he and his men should be treated fairly like good prisoners of war. This pledge was redeemed; for it was not the English, as it was the Spanish custom, to convert captives into slaves, but only to hold them for ransom. Valdez responded to Drake's politeness by kissing his hand, embracing him, and overpowering him with magnificent compliments. He was then sent on board the Lord Admiral, who received him with similar urbanity, and exprest his regret that so distinguished a personage should have been so coolly deserted by the Duke of Medina. Don Pedro then returned to the *Revenge*, where, as the guest of Drake, he was a witness to all subsequent events up to the 10th of August; on which day he was sent to London with some other officers, Sir Francis claiming his ransom as his lawful due.

Here certainly was no very triumphant beginning

for the Invincible Armada. On the very first day of their being in presence of the English fleet—then but sixty-seven in number, and vastly their inferior in size and weight of metal—they had lost the flagships of the Guipuzcoan and of the Andalusian squadrons, with a general-admiral, four hundred and fifty officers and men, and some one hundred thousand ducats of treasure. They had been outmaneuvered, outsailed, and thoroughly maltreated by their antagonists, and they had been unable to inflict a single blow in return. Thus the "small fight" had been a cheerful one for the opponents of the Inquisition, and the English were proportionally encouraged. . . . .

Never, since England was England, had such a sight been seen as now revealed itself in those narrow straits between Dover and Calais. Along that long, low, sandy shore, and quite within the range of the Calais fortifications, one hundred and thirty Spanish ships—the greater number of them the largest and most heavily armed in the world—lay face to face, and scarcely out of cannon-shot, with one hundred and fifty English sloops and frigates, the strongest and swiftest that the island could furnish, and commanded by men whose exploits had rung through the world.

Farther along the coast, invisible, but known to be performing a most perilous and vital service, was a squadron of Dutch vessels of all sizes, lining both the inner and outer edges of the sandbanks off the Flemish coasts, and swarming in all the estuaries and inlets of that intricate and dangerous cruising-ground between Dunkirk and Walcheren. Those fleets of Holland and Zeeland, numbering some one hundred and fifty galleons, sloops, and fly-boats, under Warmond, Nassau, Van der Does, De Moor, and Rosendael, lay patiently blockading every possible egress from Newport, or Gravelines, or Sluys, or Flushing, or Dunkirk; and longing to grapple with the Duke of Parma, so soon as his fleet of gunboats and hoys, packed with his Spanish and Italian veterans, should venture to set forth upon the sea for their long-prepared exploit.

It was a pompous spectacle that midsummer night upon those narrow seas. The moon, which was at the full, was rising calmly upon a scene of anxious expectation. Would she not be looking, by the morrow's night, upon a subjugated England, a reenslaved Holland—upon the downfall of civil and religious liberty? Those ships of Spain, which lay there with their banners waving in the moonlight, discharging salvos of anticipated triumph and filling the air with strains of insolent music—would they not, by daybreak, be moving straight to their purpose, bearing the conquerors of the world to the scene of their cherished hopes?

That English fleet, too, which rode there at anchor, so anxiously on the watch—would that swarm of nimble, lightly handled, but slender vessels, which had held their own hitherto in hurried and desultory skirmishes, be able to cope with their great antagonist, now that the moment had arrived for the death grapple? Would not Howard, Drake, Frobisher, Seymour, Winter, and Hawkins be swept out of the straits at last, yielding an open passage to Medina, Oquendo,

Recalde, and Farnese? Would those Hollanders and Zeelanders cruising so vigilantly among their treacherous shallows dare to maintain their post now that the terrible "Holoferness," with his invincible legions, was resolved to come forth?

And the impatience of the soldiers and sailors on board the fleet was equal to that of their commanders. There was London almost before their eyes—a huge mass of treasure, richer and more accessible than those mines beyond the Atlantic which had so often rewarded Spanish chivalry with fabulous wealth. And there were men in those galleons who remembered the sack of Antwerp eleven years before; men who could tell, from personal experience, how helpless was a great commercial city when once in the clutch of disciplined brigands; men who in that dread "fury of Antwerp" had enriched themselves in an hour with the accumulations of a merchant's lifetime, and who had slain fathers and mothers, sons and daughters, brides and bridegrooms, before each other's eyes, until the number of inhabitants butchered in the blazing streets rose to many thousands, and the plunder from palaces and warehouses was counted by millions, before the sun had set on the "great fury." Those Spaniards, and Italians, and Walloons were now thirsting for more gold, for more blood; and as the capital of England was even more wealthy and far more defenseless than the commercial metropolis of the Netherlands had been, so it was resolved that the London "fury" should be more thorough and more productive than the "fury of Antwerp," at the memory of which the world still shuddered. And these professional soldiers had been taught to consider the English as a pacific, delicate, effeminate race; dependent on good living, without experience of war, quickly fatigued and discouraged, and even more easily to be plundered and butchered than were the excellent burghers of Antwerp.

And so these southern conquerors looked down from their great galleons and galeasses upon the English vessels. More than three-quarters of them were merchantmen. There was no comparison whatever between the relative strength of the fleets. In number they were about equal, being each from one hundred and thirty to one hundred and fifty strong; but the Spaniards had twice the tonnage of the English, four times the artillery, and nearly three times the number of men. . . .

As the twilight deepened, the moon became totally obscured, dark cloud masses spread over the heavens, the sea grew black, distant thunder rolled, and the sob of an approaching tempest became distinctly audible. Such indications of a westerly gale were not encouraging to those cumbrous vessels, with the treacherous quicksands of Flanders under their lee.

At an hour past midnight it was so dark that it was difficult for the most practised eye to pierce far into the gloom. But a faint drip of oars now struck the ears of the Spaniards as they watched from the decks. A few moments afterward the sea became suddenly luminous; and six flaming vessels appeared at a slight distance, bearing steadily down upon them before the wind and tide.

There were men in the Armada who had been

at the siege of Antwerp only three years before.
They remembered with horror the devil-ships of
Gianibelli—those floating volcanoes which had
seemed to rend earth and ocean, whose explosion
had laid so many thousands of soldiers dead at
a blow, and which had shattered the bridge and
floating forts of Farnese as tho they had been
toys of glass. They knew too that the famous
engineer was at that moment in England.

In a moment one of those horrible panics which
spread with such contagious rapidity among large
bodies of men, seized upon the Spaniards. There
was a yell throughout the fleet—"The fire-ships
of Antwerp! the fire-ships of Antwerp!" and
in an instant every cable was cut, and frantic
attempts were made by each galleon and galeasse
to escape what seemed imminent destruction.
The confusion was beyond description. Four or
five of the largest ships became entangled with
each other. Two others were set on fire by the
flaming vessels and were consumed. Medina Sidonia, who had been warned, even before his
departure from Spain, that some such artifice
would probably be attempted, and who had even,
early that morning, sent out a party of sailors in
a pinnace to search for indications of the
scheme, was not surprized or dismayed. He gave
orders—as well as might be—that every ship,
after the danger should be passed, was to return
to its post and await his further orders. But
it was useless in that moment of unreasonable
panic to issue commands. The despised Man-
tuan, who had met with so many rebuffs at
Philip's court, and who—owing to official incredulity—had been but partially successful in

his magnificent enterprise at Antwerp, had now, by the mere terror of his name, inflicted more damage on Philip's Armada than had hitherto been accomplished by Howard and Drake, Hawkins and Frobisher combined.

So long as night and darkness lasted, the confusion and uproar continued. When the Monday morning dawned, several of the Spanish vessels lay disabled, while the rest of the fleet was seen at a distance of two leagues from Calais, driving toward the Flemish coast. The threatened gale had not yet begun to blow; but there were fresh squalls from the W. S. W., which, to such awkward sailors as the Spanish vessels, were difficult to contend with. On the other hand, the English fleet were all astir, and ready to pursue the Spaniards, now rapidly drifting into the North Sea.

III

"THE SPANISH FURY"[8]
(1576)

MEANTIME, while the short November day was fast declining, the combat still raged in the interior of the city (Antwerp). Various currents of conflict, forcing their separate way through many streets, had at last mingled in the Grande Place. Around this irregular, not very

---

[8] From Part IV of Chapter V of "The Rise of the Dutch Republic." Published by Harper & Brothers. The name "Spanish Fury" was given to the sack of Antwerp by the Spaniards.

spacious square, stood the gorgeous Hotel de Ville, and the tall, many-storied, fantastically gabled, richly decorated palaces of the guilds. Here a long struggle took place. It was terminated for a time by the cavalry of Vargas, who, arriving through the streets of Saint Joris, accompanied by the traitor Van Ende, charged decisively into the mêlée. The masses were broken, but multitudes of armed men found refuge in the buildings, and every house became a fortress. From every window and balcony a hot fire was poured into the square, as, pent in a corner, the burghers stood at last at bay. It was difficult to carry the houses by storm, but they were soon set on fire. A large number of sutlers and other varlets had accompanied the Spaniards from the citadel, bringing torches and kindling materials for the express purpose of firing the town. With great dexterity, these means were now applied, and in a brief interval the city hall and other edifices on the square were in flames. The conflagration spread with rapidity, house after house, street after street, taking fire. Nearly a thousand buildings, in the most splendid and wealthy quarter of the city, were soon in a blaze, and multitudes of human beings were burned with them. In the city hall many were consumed, while others leapt from the windows to renew the combat below. The many tortuous streets which led down a slight descent from the rear of the town-house to the quays were all one vast conflagration. On the other side, the magnificent cathedral, separated from the Grande Place by a single row of buildings, was lighted up, but not attacked by the flames.

The tall spire cast its gigantic shadow across the last desperate conflict. In the street called the Canal au Sucre, immediately behind the townhouse, there was a fierce struggle, a horrible massacre. A crowd of burghers, grave magistrates, and such of the German soldiers as remained alive still confronted the ferocious Spaniards. There, amid the flaming desolation, Goswyn Verreyck, the heroic margrave of the city, fought with the energy of hatred and despair. The burgomaster Van der Meere lay dead at his feet; senators, soldiers, citizens fell fast around him, and he sank at last upon a heap of slain. With him effectual resistance ended. The remaining combatants were butchered, or were slowly forced downward to perish in the Scheld. Women, children, old men were killed in countless numbers, and still, through all this havoc, directly over the heads of the struggling throng, suspended in mid-air above the din and smoke of the conflict, there sounded, every half-quarter of every hour, as if in gentle mockery, from the belfry of the cathedral, the tender and melodious chimes.

Never was there a more monstrous massacre, even in the blood-stained history of the Netherlands. It was estimated that, in the course of this and the two following days, not less than eight thousand human beings were murdered. The Spaniards seemed to cast off even the vizard of humanity. Hell seemed emptied of its fiends. Night fell upon the scene before the soldiers were masters of the city; but worse horrors began after the contest was ended. This army of brigands had come thither with a definite, practical purpose, for it was not blood-thirst, nor lust, nor revenge, which had impelled them, but it was avarice, greediness for gold. For gold they had waded through all this blood and fire. Never had men more simplicity of purpose, more directness in its execution. They had conquered their India at last; its golden mines lay all before them, and every sword should open a shaft. Riot and rape might be deferred; even murder, tho congenial to their taste, was only subsidiary to their business. They had come to take possession of the city's wealth, and they set themselves faithfully to accomplish their task. For gold, infants were dashed out of existence in their mothers' arms; for gold, parents were tortured in their children's presence; for gold, brides were scourged to death before their husbands' eyes. Wherever treasure was suspected, every expedient which ingenuity, sharpened by greediness, could suggest, was employed to extort it from its possessors. The fire, spreading more extensively and more rapidly than had been desired through the wealthiest quarter of the city, had unfortunately devoured a vast amount of property. Six millions, at least, had thus been swallowed; a destruction by which no one had profited. There was, however, much left. The strong boxes of the merchants, the gold, silver, and precious jewelry, the velvets, satins, brocades, laces, and similar well concentrated and portable plunder, were rapidly appropriated. So far the course was plain and easy, but in private houses it was more difficult. The cash, plate, and other valuables of individuals were not so easily discovered.

Torture was, therefore, at once employed to discover the hidden treasures. After all had been given, if the sum seemed too little, the proprietors were brutally punished for their poverty or their supposed dissimulation. A gentlewoman, named Fabry, with her aged mother and other females of the family, had taken refuge in the cellar of her mansion. As the day was drawing to a close, a band of plunderers entered, who, after ransacking the house, descended to the cellarage. Finding the door barred, they forced it open with gunpowder. The mother, who was nearest the entrance, fell dead on the threshold. Stepping across her mangled body, the brigands sprang upon her daughter, loudly demanding the property which they believed to be concealed. They likewise insisted on being informed where the master of the house had taken refuge. Protestations of ignorance as to hidden treasure, or the whereabouts of her husband, who, for aught she knew, was lying dead in the streets, were of no avail. To make her more communicative, they hanged her on a beam in the cellar, and after a few moments cut her down before life was extinct. Still receiving no satisfactory reply, where a satisfactory reply was impossible, they hanged her again. Again, after another brief interval, they gave her a second release, and a fresh interrogatory. This barbarity they repeated several times, till they were satisfied that there was nothing to be gained by it, while, on the other hand, they were losing much valuable time. Hoping to be more successful elsewhere, they left her hanging for the last time, and trooped off to fresher fields. Strange to

relate, the person thus horribly tortured survived.
A servant in her family, married to a Spanish
soldier, providentially entered the house in time
to rescue her perishing mistress. She was restored to existence, but never to reason. Her
brain was hopelessly crazed, and she passed the
remainder of her life wandering about her house,
or feebly digging in her garden for the buried
treasure which she had been thus fiercely solicited
to reveal.

A wedding-feast was rudely interrupted. Two
young persons, neighbors of opulent families, had
been long betrothed, and the marriage-day had
been fixt for Sunday, the fatal 4th of November.
The guests were assembled, the ceremony concluded, and the nuptial banquet in progress, when
the horrible outcries in the streets proclaimed
that the Spaniards had broken loose. Hour after
hour of trembling expectation succeeded. At
last, a thundering at the gate proclaimed the
arrival of a band of brigands. Preceded by their
captain, a large number of soldiers forced their
way into the house, ransacking every chamber,
no opposition being offered by the family and
friends, too few and powerless to cope with this
band of well-armed ruffians. Plate chests, ward-
robes, desks, caskets of jewelry were freely offered, eagerly accepted, but not found sufficient,
and to make the luckless wretches furnish more
than they possest, the usual brutalities were employed. The soldiers began by striking the bride-
groom dead. The bride fell shrieking into her
mother's arms, whence she was torn by the murderers, who immediately put the mother to death,
and an indiscriminate massacre then followed

the fruitless attempts to obtain by threats and torture treasure which did not exist. The bride, who was of remarkable beauty, was carried off to the citadel. Maddened by this last outrage, the father, who was the only man of the party left alive, rushed upon the Spaniards. Wresting a sword from one of the crew, the old man dealt with it so fiercely that he stretched more than one enemy dead at his feet, but it is needless to add that he was soon dispatched.

Meantime, while the party were concluding the plunder of the mansion, the bride was left in a lonely apartment of the fortress. Without wasting time in fruitless lamentation, she resolved to quit the life which a few hours had made so desolate. She had almost succeeded in hanging herself with a massive gold chain which she wore, when her captor entered the apartment. Inflamed, not with lust, but with avarice, excited not by her charms, but by her jewelry, he rescued her from her perilous position. He then took possession of her chain and the other trinkets with which her wedding-dress was adorned, and caused her to be entirely stript of her clothing. She was then scourged with rods till her beautiful body was bathed in blood, and at last alone, naked, nearly mad, was sent back into the city. Here the forlorn creature wandered up and down through the blazing streets, among the heaps of dead and dying, till she was at last put out of her misery by a gang of soldiers.

Such are a few isolated instances, accidentally preserved in their details, of the general horrors inflicted on this occasion. Others innumerable have sunk into oblivion. On the morning of the 5th of

November Antwerp presented a ghastly sight. The magnificent marble town-house, celebrated as a "world's wonder," even in that age and country, in which so much splendor was lavished on municipal palaces, stood a blackened ruin— all but the walls destroyed, while its archives, accounts, and other valuable contents had perished. The more splendid portion of the city had been consumed, at least five hundred palaces, mostly of marble or hammered stone, being a smoldering mass of destruction. The dead bodies of those fallen in the massacre were on every side, in greatest profusion around the Place de Meer, among the Gothic pillars of the Exchange, and in the streets near the town-house. The German soldiers lay in their armor, some with their heads burned from their bodies, some with legs and arms consumed by the flames through which they had fought. The Margrave Goswyn Verreyck, the burgomaster Van der Meere, the magistrates Lancelot Van Urselen, Nicholas Van Boekholt, and other leading citizens lay among piles of less distinguished slain. They remained unburied until the overseers of the poor, on whom the living had then more importunate claims than the dead, were compelled by Roda to bury them out of the pauper fund. The murderers were too thrifty to be at funeral charges for their victims. The ceremony was not hastily performed, for the number of corpses had not been completed. Two days longer the havoc lasted in the city. Of all the crimes which men can commit, whether from deliberate calculation or in the frenzy of passion, hardly one was omitted, for riot, gaming, rape, which had been postponed to the more stringent claims of robbery and murder, were now rapidly added to the sum of atrocities. History has recorded the account indelibly on her brazen tablets; it can be adjusted only at the judgment-seat above.

Of all the deeds of darkness yet compassed in the Netherlands this was the worst. It was called The Spanish Fury, by which dread name it has been known for ages. The city, which had been a world of wealth and splendor, was changed to a charnel-house, and from that hour its commercial prosperity was blasted. Other causes had silently girdled the yet green and flourishing tree, but the Spanish Fury was the fire which consumed it to ashes. Three thousand dead bodies were discovered in the streets, as many more were estimated to have perished in the Scheld, and nearly an equal number were burned or destroyed in other ways. Eight thousand persons undoubtedly were put to death. Six millions of property were destroyed by the fire, and at least as much more was obtained by the Spaniards.

RICHARD HENRY DANA
THE YOUNGER

Born in Cambridge, Mass., in 1815: died in 1882; being in ill health, shipped before the mast in 1834, making a voyage to the Pacific, described in his book "Two Years Before the Mast," published in 1840; one of the founders of the Free Soil party in 1848; edited Wheaton's "Elements of International Law," published in 1866.

A FIERCE GALE UNDER A CLEAR SKY [1]

WE had been below but a short time before we had the usual premonitions of a coming gale —seas washing over the whole forward part of the vessel, and her bows beating against them with a force and sound like the driving of piles. The watch, too, seemed very busy trampling about decks and singing out at the ropes. A sailor can tell by the sound what sail is coming in; and in a short time we heard the top-gallant-sails come in, one after another, and then the flying jib. This seemed to ease her a good deal, and we were fast going off to the land of Nod, when—bang, bang, bang on the scuttle, and "All hands, reef topsails, ahoy!" started us out of our berths, and it not being very cold weather, we had nothing extra to put on, and were soon on deck.

I shall never forget the fineness of the sight. It was a clear and rather a chilly night; the stars were twinkling with an intense brightness, and as far as the eye could reach there was not

[1] From "Two Years Before the Mast."

a cloud to be seen. The horizon met the sea in a defined line. A painter could not have painted so clear a sky. There was not a speck upon it. Yet it was blowing great guns from the northwest. When you can see a cloud to windward, you feel that there is a place for the wind to come from; but here it seemed to come from nowhere. No person could have told from the heavens, by their eyesight alone, that it was not a still summer's night. One reef after another we took in the topsails, and before we could get them hoisted up we heard a sound like a short quick rattling of thunder, and the jib was blown to atoms out of the bolt-rope. We got the topsails set, and the fragments of the jib stowed away, and the foretopmast staysail set in its place, when the great mainsail gaped open, and the sail ripped from head to foot. "Lay up on that main yard and furl the sail, before it blows to tatters!" shouted the captain; and in a moment we were up, gathering the remains of it upon the yard. We got it wrapt round the yard, and passed gaskets over it as snugly as possible, and were just on deck again, when with another loud rent, which was heard throughout the ship, the foretopsail, which had been double-reefed, split in two athwartships, just below the reef-band, from earing to earing. Here again it was—down yard, haul out reef-tackles, and lay out upon the yard for reefing. By hauling the reef-tackles chock-a-block we took the strain from the other earings, and passing the close-reef earing, and knotting the points carefully, we succeeded in setting the sail, close reefed.

We had but just got the rigging coiled up, and were waiting to hear "Go below the watch!" when the main royal worked loose from the gaskets, and blew directly out to leeward, flapping and shaking the mast like a wand. Here was a job for somebody. The royal must come in or be cut adrift, or the mast would be snapt short off. All the light hands in the starboard watch were sent up one after another, but they could do nothing with it. At length John, the tall Frenchman, the head of the starboard watch (and a better sailor never stept upon a deck), sprang aloft, and by the help of his long arms and legs succeeded after a hard struggle—the sail blowing over the yard-arm to leeward, and the skysail adrift directly over his head—in smothering it and frapping it with long pieces of sinnet. He came very near being blown or shaken from the yard several times, but he was a true sailor, every finger a fish-hook. Having made the sail snug, he prepared to send the yard down, which was a long and difficult job; for frequently he was obliged to stop and hold on with all his might for several minutes, the ship pitching so as to make it impossible to do anything else at that height. The yard at length came down safe, and after it the fore and mizzen royal yards were sent down. All hands were then sent aloft, and for an hour or two we were hard at work, making the booms well fast, unreefing the studding sail and royal and skysail gear, getting rolling-ropes on the yard, setting up the weather breast-backstays, and making other preparations for a storm. It was a fine night for a gale, just cool and bracing enough for quick work, without being cold, and as bright as day. It was sport to have a gale in such weather as this. Yet it blew like a hurricane. The wind seemed to come with a spite, an edge to it, which threatened to scrape us off the yards. The force of the wind was greater than I had ever felt it before; but darkness, cold, and wet are the worst parts of a storm to a sailor.

Having got on deck again, we looked round to see what time of night it was, and whose watch. In a few minutes the man at the wheel struck four bells, and we found that the other watch was out and our own half out. Accordingly, the starboard watch went below, and left the ship to us for a couple of hours, yet with orders to stand by for a call.

Hardly had they got below before away went the foretopmast staysail, blown to ribbons. This was a small sail, which we could manage in the watch, so that we were not obliged to call up the other watch. We laid upon the bowsprit, where we were under water half the time, and took in the fragments of the sail; and as she must have some headsail on her, prepared to bend another staysail. We got the new one out into the nettings; seized on the tack, sheets, and halyards, and the hanks; manned the halyards, cut adrift the frapping-lines, and hoisted away; but before it was half-way up the stay it was blown all to pieces. When we belayed the halyards, there was nothing left but the bolt-rope. Now large eyes began to show themselves in the foresail; and knowing that it must soon go, the mate ordered us upon the yard to furl it. Being unwilling to call up the watch, who had been on deck all night, he roused out the carpenter, sailmaker, cook, and steward, and with their help we manned the foreyard, and after nearly half an hour's struggle, mastered the sail and got it well furled round the yard.

The force of the wind had never been greater than at this moment. In going up the rigging it seemed absolutely to pin us down to the shrouds; and on the yard there was no such thing as turning a face to windward. Yet there was no driving sleet and darkness and wet and cold as off Cape Horn; and instead of stiff oilcloth suits, southwester caps, and thick boots, we had on hats, round jackets, duck trousers, light shoes, and everything light and easy. These things make a great difference to a sailor. When we got on deck the man at the wheel struck eight bells (four o'clock in the morning), and "All starbowlines, ahoy!" brought the other watch up, but there was no going below for us. The gale was now at its height, "blowing like scissors and thumb-screws"; the captain was on deck; the ship, which was light, rolling and pitching as tho she would shake the long sticks out of her, and the sails were gaping open and splitting in every direction. The mizzen-topsail, which was a comparatively new sail and close reefed, split from head to foot in the bunt; the foretopsail went in one rent from clew to earing, and was blowing to tatters; one of the chain bobstays parted; the spritsailyard sprung in the slings, the martingale had slued away off to leeward; and owing to the long dry weather the lee rigging hung in large bights at every lurch. One of the main-topgallant shrouds had parted; and to crown all, the galley had got adrift and gone over to leeward, and the anchor on the lee bow had worked loose and was thumping the side. Here was work enough for all hands for half a day. Our gang laid out on the mizzen-top-sailyard, and after more than half an hour's hard work furled the sail, tho it bellied out over our heads, and again, by a slat of the wind, blew in under the yard with a fearful jerk and almost threw us off from the foot-ropes. . . .

It was now eleven o'clock, and the watch was sent below to get breakfast, and at eight bells (noon), as everything was snug, altho the gale had not in the least abated, the watch was set and the other watch and idlers sent below. For three days and three nights the gale continued with unabated fury, and with singular regularity. There were no lulls, and very little variation in its fierceness. Our ship, being light, rolled so as almost to send the fore yard-arm under water, and drifted off bodily to leeward. All this time there was not a cloud to be seen in the sky, day or night; no, not so large as a man's hand. Every morning the sun rose cloudless from the sea, and set again at night in the sea in a flood of light. The stars, too, came out of the blue one after another, night after night, unobscured, and twinkled as clear as on a still frosty night at home, until the day came upon them. All this time the sea was rolling in immense surges, white with foam, as far as the eye could reach, on every side; for we were now leagues and leagues from shore.

HENRY DAVID THOREAU

Born in Concord, Mass., in 1817; died in 1862; graduated from Harvard in 1837; taught school; practised surveying; lived alone at Walden Pond in 1845-47; a friend of Emerson and Alcott; imprisoned for refusal to pay a tax he believed to be unjust; published "A Week on the Concord and Merrimac Rivers" in 1849, and "Walden" in 1854; "Excursions" published after his death, with a memoir, by Emerson, "The Maine Woods" in 1864, "Cape Cod" in 1865; his "Journals" and other works also published after his death.

I

THE BUILDING OF HIS HOUSE AT WALDEN POND [1]

WHEN I wrote the following pages, or rather the bulk of them, I lived alone, in the woods, a mile from any neighbor, in a house which I had built myself, on the shore of Walden Pond, in Concord, Massachusetts, and earned my living by the labor of my hands only. I lived there two years and two months. At present I am a sojourner in civilized life again. . . .

Near the end of March, 1845, I borrowed an ax and went down to the woods by Walden Pond, nearest to where I intended to build my house, and began to cut down some tall arrowy white

[1] From Chapter I of "Walden, or Life in the Woods."

pines, still in their youth, for timber. It is difficult to begin without borrowing, but perhaps it is the most generous course thus to permit your fellow men to have an interest in your enterprise. The owner of the ax, as he released his hold on it, said that it was the apple of his eye; but I returned it sharper than I received it. It was a pleasant hillside where I worked, covered with pine woods, through which I looked out on the pond, and a small open field in the woods where pines and hickories were springing up. The ice in the pond was not yet dissolved, tho there were some open spaces, and it was all dark colored and saturated with water. There were some slight flurries of snow during the days that I worked there; but for the most part when I came out on to the railroad, on my way home, its yellow sand heap stretched away gleaming in the hazy atmosphere, and the rails shone in the spring sun, and I heard the lark and pewee and other birds already come to commence another year with us. . . .

I hewed the main timbers six inches square, most of the studs on two sides only, and the rafters and floor timbers on one side, leaving the rest of the bark on, so that they were just as straight and much stronger than sawed ones. Each stick was carefully mortised or tenoned by its stump, for I had borrowed other tools by this time. My days in the woods were not very long ones; yet I usually carried my dinner of bread and butter, and read the newspaper in which it was wrapt, at noon, sitting amid the green pine boughs which I had cut off, and to my bread was imparted some of their fragrance,

for my hands were covered with a thick coat of
pitch. Before I had done I was more the friend
than the foe of the pine-tree, tho I had cut down
some of them, having become better acquainted with it. Sometimes a rambler in the wood
was attracted by the sound of my ax, and we
chatted pleasantly over the chips which I had
made. . . .

I dug my cellar in the side of a hill sloping
to the south, where a woodchuck had formerly
dug his burrow, down through sumac and black-
berry roots, and the lowest stain of vegetation,
six feet square by seven deep, to a fine sand
where potatoes would not freeze in any winter.
The sides were left shelving, and not stoned;
but the sun having never shone on them, the
sand still keeps its place. It was but two hours'
work. I took particular pleasure in this breaking
of ground, for in almost all latitudes men dig
into the earth for an equable temperature. Under
the most splendid house in the city is still to be
found the cellar where they store their roots
as of old, and long after the superstructure has
disappeared posterity will remark its dent in the
earth. The house is still but a sort of porch at
the entrance of a burrow.

At length, in the beginning of May, with the
help of some of my acquaintances, rather to im-
prove so good an occasion for neighborliness than
from any necessity, I set up the frame of my
house. No man was ever more honored in the
character of his raisers than I. They are destined, I trust, to assist at the raising of loftier
structures one day. I began to occupy my house
on the 4th of July, as soon as it was boarded

and roofed, for the boards were carefully feather-edged and lapped, so that it was perfectly impervious to rain; but before boarding I laid the foundation of a chimney at one end, bringing two cartloads of stones up the hill from the pond in my arms. I built the chimney after my hoeing in the fall, before a fire became necessary for warmth, doing my cooking in the meanwhile out-of-doors, on the ground, early in the morning; which mode I still think is in some respects more convenient and agreeable than the usual one. When it stormed before my bread was baked, I fixt a few boards over the fire, and sat under them to watch my loaf, and passed some pleasant hours in that way. In those days, when my hands were much employed, I read but little, but the least scraps of paper which lay on the ground, my holder, or tablecloth, afforded me as much entertainment, in fact, answered the same purpose as the Iliad.

Before winter I built a chimney, and shingled the sides of my house, which were already impervious to rain, with imperfect and sappy shingles made of the first slice of the log, which edges I was obliged to straighten with a plane.

I have thus a tight shingled and plastered house, ten feet wide by fifteen long, and eight-feet posts, with a garret and a closet, a large window on each side, two trap doors, one door at the end, and a brick fireplace opposite. The exact cost of my house, paying the usual price for such materials as I used, but not counting the work, all of which was done by myself, was as follows; and I give the details because very few are able to tell exactly what their houses cost, and fewer still, if any, the separate cost of the various materials which compose them:

Boards	$ 8.03½
Refuse shingles for roof and sides	4.00
Laths	1.25
Two second-hand windows with glass	2.43
One thousand old brick	4.00
Two casks of lime (That was high)	2.40
Hair (More than I needed)	0.31
Mantle-tree iron	0.15
Nails	3.90
Hinges and screws	0.14
Latch	0.10
Chalk	0.01
Transportation (I carried a good part on my back)	1.40
In all	$28.12½

These are all the materials excepting the timber, stones, and sand, which I claimed by squatter's right. I have also a small woodshed adjoining, made chiefly of the stuff which was left after building the house.

II

HOW TO MAKE TWO SMALL ENDS MEET[2]

BEFORE I finished my house, wishing to earn ten or twelve dollars by some honest and agreeable method, in order to meet my unusual expenses, I planted about two acres and a half of light and sandy soil near it chiefly with beans,

[2]From Chapters I and II of "Walden."

but also a small part with potatoes, corn, peas, and turnips. The whole lot contains eleven acres, mostly growing up to pines and hickories, and was sold the preceding season for eight dollars and eight cents an acre. One farmer said that it was "good for nothing but to raise cheeping squirrels on." I put no manure whatever on this land, not being the owner, but merely a squatter, and not expecting to cultivate so much again, and I did not quite hoe it all once. I got out several cords of stumps in plowing, which supplied me with fuel for a long time, and left small circles of virgin mold, easily distinguishable through the summer by the greater luxuriance of the beans there. The dead and for the most part unmerchantable wood behind my house, and the driftwood from the pond, have supplied the remainder of my fuel. I was obliged to hire a team and a man for the plowing, tho I held the plow myself. My farm outgoes for the first season were, for implements, seed, work, etc., $14.72½. The seed corn was given me. This never costs anything to speak of, unless you plant more than enough. I got twelve bushels of beans, and eighteen bushels of potatoes, besides some peas and sweet corn. The yellow corn and turnips were too late to come to anything. My whole income from the farm was

$23.44

Deducting the outgoes 14.72½

There are left .... $ 8.71½

besides produce consumed and on hand at the time this estimate was made of the value of $4.50—the amount on hand much more than balancing a little grass which I did not raise. All things considered, that is considering the importance of a man's soul and of to-day, notwithstanding the short time occupied by my experiment, nay, partly even because of its transient character I believe that that was doing better than any farmer in Concord did that year.

The next year I did better still, for I spaded up all the land which I required, about a third of an acre, and I learned from the experience of both years, not being in the least awed by many celebrated works on husbandry, Arthur Young among the rest, that if one would live simply and eat only the crop which he raised, and raise no more than he ate, and not exchange it for an insufficient quantity of more luxurious and expensive things, he would need to cultivate only a few rods of ground, and that it would be cheaper to spade up than than to use oxen to plow it, and to select a fresh spot from time to time than to manure the old, and he could do all his necessary farm work as it were with his left hand at odd hours in the summer; and thus he would not be tied to an ox, or horse, or cow, or pig, as at present. I desire to speak impartially on this point, and as one not interested in the success or failure of the present economical and social arrangements. I was more independent than any farmer in Concord, for I was not anchored to a house or farm, but could follow the bent of my genius, which is a very crooked one, every moment. Besides being better off than they already, if my house had been burned or my crops had failed, I should have been nearly as well off as before. . . .

By surveying, carpentry, and day-labor of various other kinds in the village in the meanwhile, for I have as many trades as fingers, I had earned $13.34. The expense of food for eight months, namely, from July 4th to March 1st, the time when these estimates were made, tho I lived there more than two years — not counting potatoes, a little green corn, and some peas, which I had raised, nor considering the value of what was on hand at the last date, was

Rice $1.73½	
Molasses (Cheapest form of the saccharine) .. 1.73	
Rye meal 1.04¾	
Indian meal (Cheaper than rye) 0.99¾	
Pork 0.22	All
Flour (Costs more than Indian meal, both money and trouble) .. 0.88	Experiments which had failed
Sugar 0.80	
Lard 0.65	
Apples 0.25	
Dried apple 0.22	
Sweet potatoes 0.10	
One pumpkin 0.06	
One watermelon 0.02	
Salt 0.03	

Yes, I did eat $8.74, all told; but I should not thus unblushingly publish my guilt, if I did not know that most of my readers were equally guilty with myself, and that their deeds would look no better in print. The next year I sometimes caught a mess of fish for my dinner, and once I went so far as to slaughter a woodchuck which ravaged my beanfield—effect his transmigration, as a Tartar would say—and devour him, partly for experiment's sake; but tho it afforded me a momentary enjoyment, notwithstanding a musky flavor, I saw that the longest use would not make that a good practise, however it might seem to have your woodchucks ready drest by the village butcher.

Clothing and some incidental expenses within the same date, tho little can be inferred from this item, amounted to

	$8.40¾
Oil and some household utensils.........	2.00

So that all the pecuniary outgoes, excepting for washing and mending, which for the most part were done out of the house, and their bills have not yet been received—and these are all and more than all the ways by which money necessarily goes out in this part of the world—were

House	$28.12½
Farm, one year	14.72½
Food, eight months	8.74
Clothing, etc., eight months	8.40¾
Oil, etc., eight months	2.00
In all	$61.99¾

I address myself now to those of my readers who have a living to get. And to meet this I have for farm produce sold

	$23.44
Earned by day-labor	13.34
In all	$36.78

which subtracted from the sum of the outgoes leaves a balance of $25.21¾ on the one side, this being very nearly the means with which I started, and the measure of expenses to be incurred—

and on the other, besides the leisure and independence and health thus secured, a comfortable house for me as long as I choose to occupy it.

These statistics, however accidental and therefore uninstructive they may appear, as they have a certain completeness, have a certain value also. Nothing was given me of which I have not rendered some account. It appears from the above estimate that my food alone cost me in money about twenty-seven cents a week. It was, for nearly two years after this, rye and Indian meal without yeast, potatoes, rice, a very little salt pork, molasses, and salt, and my drink water. It was fit that I should live on rice, mainly, who loved so well the philosophy of India. To meet the objections of some inveterate cavillers, I may as well state that if I dined out occasionally, as I always had done, and I trust shall have opportunities to do again, it was frequently to the detriment of my domestic arrangements. But the dining out, being, as I have stated, a constant element, does not in the least affect a comparative statement like this.

I learned from my two years' experience that it would cost incredibly little trouble to obtain one's necessary food, even in this latitude; that a man may use as simple a diet as the animals, and yet retain health and strength. I have made a satisfactory dinner, satisfactory on several accounts, simply off a dish of purslane (*Portulaca Oleracea*) which I gathered in my cornfield, boiled and salted. I give the Latin on account of the savoriness of the trivial name. And pray what more can a reasonable man desire, in peaceful times, in ordinary noons, than sufficient number of ears of green sweet-corn boiled, with the addition of salt? Even the little variety which I used was a yielding to the demands of appetite, and not of health. Yet men have come to such a pass that they frequently starve, not for want of necessaries, but for want of luxuries; and I know a good woman who thinks that her son lost his life because he took to drinking water only.

The reader will perceive that I am treating the subject rather from an economic than a dietetic point of view, and he will not venture to put my abstemiousness to the test unless he has a well-stocked larder.

Bread I at first made of pure Indian meal and salt, genuine hoe-cakes, which I baked before my fire out of doors on a shingle or the end of a stick of timber sawed off in building my house; but it was wont to get smoked and to have a piny flavor. I tried flour also; but have at last found a mixture of rye and Indian meal most convenient and agreeable. In cold weather it was no little amusement to bake several small loaves of this in succession, tending and turning them as carefully as an Egyptian his hatching eggs. They were a real cereal fruit which I ripened, and they had to my senses a fragrance like that of other noble fruits, which I kept in as long as possible by wrapping them in cloths. I made a study of the ancient and indispensable art of bread-making, consulting such authorities as offered, going back to the primitive days and first invention of the unleavened kind, when from the wildness of nuts and meats men first reached the mildness and refinement of this diet, and traveling gradually down in my studies through that accidental souring of the dough, which, it is supposed, taught the leavening process, and through the various fermentations thereafter, till I came to "good, sweet, wholesome bread," the staff of life.

For more than five years I maintained myself thus solely by the labor of my hands, and I found that by working about six weeks in a year, I could meet all the expenses of living. The whole of my winters, as well as most of my summers, I had free and clear for study. I have thoroughly tried school-keeping, and found that my expenses were in proportion, or rather out of proportion, to my income, for I was obliged to dress and train, not to say think and believe, accordingly, and I lost my time into the bargain. As I did not teach for the good of my fellow men, but simply for a livelihood, this was a failure. I have tried trade; but I found that it would take ten years to get under way in that, and that then I should probably be on my way to the devil. I was actually afraid that I might by that time be doing what is called a good business. When formerly I was looking about to see what I could do for a living, some sad experience in conforming to the wishes of friends being fresh in my mind to tax my ingenuity, I thought often and seriously of picking huckleberries; that surely I could do, and its small profits might suffice—for my greatest skill has been to want but little—so little capital it required, so little distraction from my wonted moods, I foolishly thought. While my acquaintances went unhesitatingly into trade or the professions, I contemplated this occupation as most like theirs; ranging the hills all summer to pick the berries which came in my way, and thereafter carelessly dispose of them; so to keep the flocks of Admetus. I also dreamed that I might gather the wild herbs, or carry evergreens to such villagers as loved to be reminded of the woods, even to the city, by hay-cart loads. But I have since learned that trade curses everything it handles; and tho you trade in messages from heaven, the whole curse of trade attaches to the business. . . .

In short, I am convinced, both by faith and experience, that to maintain one's self on this earth is not a hardship but a pastime, if we will live simply and wisely; as the pursuits of the simpler nations are still the sports of the more artificial. It is not necessary that a man should earn his living by the sweat of his brow, unless he sweats easier than I do. . . .

The only house I had been the owner of before, if I except a boat, was a tent, which I used occasionally when making excursions in the summer, and this is still rolled up in my garret; but the boat, after passing from hand to hand, has gone down the stream of time. With this more substantial shelter about me, I had made some progress toward settling in the world. This frame, so slightly clad, was a sort of crystallization around me, and reacted on the builder. It was suggestive as a picture in outlines. I did not need to go outdoors to take the air, for the atmosphere within had lost none of its freshness. It was not so much within doors as behind a door where I sat, even in the rainiest weather.

The Harivansa says, "An abode without birds is like a meat without seasoning." Such was not my abode, for I found myself suddenly neighbor to the birds; not by having imprisoned one, but having caged myself near them. I was not only nearer to some of those which commonly frequent the garden and the orchard, but to those wilder and more thrilling songsters of the forest which never, or rarely, serenade a villager, the wood-thrush, the veery, the scarlet tanager, the field-sparrow, the whippoorwill, and many others.

I was seated by the shore of a small pond, about a mile and a half south of the village of Concord, and somewhat higher than it, in the midst of an extensive wood between that town and Lincoln, and about two miles south of that our only field known to fame, Concord battle ground; but I was so low in the woods that the opposite shore, half a mile off, like the rest covered with wood, was my most distant horizon. For the first week, whenever I looked out on the pond it imprest me like a tarn high up on the side of a mountain, its bottom far above the surface of other lakes, and, as the sun arose, I saw it throwing off its mighty clothing of mist, and here and there, by degrees, its soft ripples or its smooth reflecting surface were revealed, while the mists, like ghosts, were stealthily withdrawing in every direction into the woods, as at the breaking up of some nocturnal conventicle. The very dew seemed to hang upon the trees later into the day than usual, as on the sides of mountains.

I went to the woods because I wished to live deliberately, to front only the essential facts of life, and see if I could not learn what it had to teach, and not, when I came to die, discover that I had not lived. I did not wish to live what was not life, living is so dear; nor did I wish to practise resignation, unless it was quite necessary. I wanted to live deep and suck out all the marrow of life, to live so sturdily and Spartan-like as to put to rout all that was not life, to cut a broad swath and shave close, to drive life into a corner, and reduce it to its lowest terms, and, if it proved to be mean, then to get the whole and genuine meanness of it, and publish its meanness to the world; or if it were sublime, to know it by experience, and be able to give a true account of it in my next excursion. For most men, it appears to me, are in a strange uncertainty about it, whether it is of the devil or of God, and have somewhat hastily concluded that it is the chief end of man here to "glorify God and enjoy Him forever."

Still we live meanly, like ants; tho the fable tells us that we were long ago changed into men; like pygmies we fight with cranes; it is error upon error, and clout upon clout, and our best virtue has for its occasion a superfluous and evitable wretchedness. Our life is frittered away by detail. An honest man has hardly need to count more than his ten fingers, or in extreme cases he may add his ten toes, and lump the rest. Simplicity, simplicity, simplicity! I say, let your affairs be as two or three, and not a hundred or a thousand; instead of a million count half a dozen, and keep your accounts on your thumb nail. In the midst of this chopping sea of civilized life, such are the clouds and storms and quicksands and thousand and one items to be allowed for that a man has to live, if he would not founder and go to the bottom and not make his port at all, by dead reckoning, and he must be a great calculator indeed who succeeds. Simplify, simplify. Instead of three meals a day, if it be necessary, eat but one; instead of a hundred dishes, five; and reduce other things in proportion.

Let us spend one day as deliberately as Nature, and not be thrown off the track by every nutshell and mosquito's wing that falls on the rails. Let us rise early and fast, or break fast, gently and without perturbation; let company come and let company go, let the bells ring and the children cry—determined to make a day of it. Why should we knock under and go with the stream? Let us not be upset and overwhelmed in that terrible rapid and whirlpool called a dinner, situated in the meridian shallows. Weather this danger and you are safe, for the rest of the way is down hill. With unrelaxed nerves, with morning vigor, sail by it, looking another way, tied to the mast like Ulysses. If the engine whistles, let it whistle till it is hoarse for its pains. If the bell rings, why should we run? We will consider what kind of music they are like.

III

ON READING THE ANCIENT CLASSICS[s]

THE student may read Homer or Æschylus in the Greek without danger of dissipation or luxuriousness, for it implies that he in some measure emulates their heroes, and consecrates morning hours to their pages. The heroic books, even if printed in the character of our mother tongue, will always be in a language dead to degenerate times; and we must laboriously seek the meaning of each word and line, conjecturing a larger sense than common use permits out of that wisdom and valor and generosity we have. The modern cheap and fertile press, with all its translations, has done little to bring us nearer to the heroic writers of antiquity. They seem as solitary, and the letter in which they are printed as rare and curious as ever. It is worth the expense of youthful days and costly hours, if you learn only some words of an ancient language, which are raised out of the trivialness of the street, to be perpetual suggestions and provocation. It is not in vain that the farmer remembers and repeats the few Latin words which he has heard. Men sometimes speak as if the study of the classics would at length make way for more modern and practical studies; but the adventurous student will always study classics, in whatever language they may be written and however ancient they may be. For what are

[s] From Chapter III of "Walden."

the classics but the noblest recorded thoughts of man? They are the only oracles which are not decayed, and there are such answers to the most modern inquiry in them as Delphi and Dodona never gave. We might as well omit to study Nature because she is old.

To read well, that is, to read true books in a true spirit, is a noble exercise, and one that will tax the reader more than any exercise which the customs of the day esteem. It requires a training such as the athletes underwent, the steady intention almost of the whole life to this object. Books must be read as deliberately and reservedly as they were written. It is not enough even to be able to speak the language of that nation by which they are written, for there is a memorable interval between the spoken and the written language, the language heard and the language read. The one is commonly transitory, a sound, a tongue, a dialect merely, almost brutish, and we learn it unconsciously, like the brutes, of our mothers. The other is the maturity and experience of that; if that is our mother tongue, this is our father tongue, a reserved and select expression, too significant to be heard by the ear, which we must be born again in order to speak. The crowds of men who merely spoke the Greek and Latin tongues in the Middle Ages were not entitled by the accident of birth to read the works of genius written in those languages; for these were not written in that Greek or Latin which they knew, but in the select language of literature. They had not learned the nobler dialects of Greece and Rome, but the very materials on which they were written were waste paper to them, and they prized instead a cheap contemporary literature. But when the several nations of Europe had acquired distinct tho rude written languages of their own, sufficient for the purposes of their rising literatures, then first learning revived, and scholars were enabled to discern from that remoteness the treasures of antiquity. What the Roman and Grecian multitude could not hear, after the lapse of ages a few scholars read, and a few scholars only are still reading it.

However much we may admire the orator's occasional bursts of eloquence, the noblest written words are commonly as far behind or above the fleeting spoken language as the firmament with its stars is behind the clouds. There are the stars, and they who can may read them. The astronomers forever comment on and observe them. They are not exhalations like our daily colloquies and vaporous breath. What is called eloquence in the forum is commonly found to be rhetoric in the study. The orator yields to the inspiration of a transient occasion, and speaks to the mob before him, to those who can hear him; but the writer, whose more equable life is his occasion, and who would be distracted by the event and the crowd which inspire the orator, speaks to the intellect and heart of mankind, to all in any age who can understand him.

No wonder that Alexander carried the Iliad with him on his expeditions in a precious casket. A written word is the choicest of relics. It is something at once more intimate with us and more universal than any other work of art. It is the work of art nearest to life itself. It may be translated into every language, and not only be read but actually breathed from all human lips; not be represented on canvas or in marble only, but be carved out of the breath of life itself. The symbol of an ancient man's thought becomes a modern man's speech. Two thousand summers have imparted to the monuments of Grecian literature, as to her marbles, only a maturer golden and autumnal tint, for they have carried their own serene and celestial atmosphere into all lands to protect them against the corrosion of time. Books are the treasured wealth of the world and the fit inheritance of generations and nations. Books, the oldest and the best, stand naturally and rightfully on the shelves of every cottage. They have no cause of their own to plead, but while they enlighten and sustain the reader his common sense will not refuse them. Their authors are a natural and irresistible aristocracy in every society, and, more than kings or emperors, exert an influence on mankind. When the illiterate and perhaps scornful trader has earned by enterprise and industry his coveted leisure and independence, and is admitted to the circles of wealth and fashion, he turns inevitably at last to those still higher but yet inaccessible circles of intellect and genius, and is sensible only of the imperfection of his culture, and the vanity and insufficiency of all his riches, and further proves his good sense by the pains which he takes to secure for his children that intellectual culture whose want he so keenly feels; and thus it is that he becomes the founder of a family.

Those who have not learned to read the ancient classics in the language in which they were written must have a very imperfect knowledge of the history of the human race; for it is remarkable that no transcript of them has ever been made into any modern tongue, unless our civilization itself may be regarded as such a transcript. Homer has never yet been printed in English, nor Æschylus, nor Virgil even—works as refined, as solidly done, and as beautiful almost as the morning itself; for later writers, say what we will of their genius, have rarely, if ever, equaled the elaborate beauty and finish and the lifelong and heroic literary labors of the ancients. They only talk of forgetting them who never knew them. It will be soon enough to forget them when we have the learning and the genius which will enable us to attend to and appreciate them. That age will be rich, indeed, when those relics which we call classics, and the still older and more than classic but even less known scriptures of the nations, shall have still further accumulated, when the Vaticans shall be filled with Vedas and Zendavestas and Bibles, with Homers and Dantes and Shakespeares, and all the centuries to come shall have successively deposited their trophies in the forum of the world. By such a pile we may hope to scale heaven at last.

IV

OF SOCIETY AND SOLITUDE [4]

WHEN I return to my house I find that visitors have been there and left their cards, either a bunch of flowers, or a wreath of evergreen, or a name in pencil on a yellow walnut leaf or a chip. They who come rarely to the woods take some little piece of the forest into their hands to play with by the way, which they leave, either intentionally or accidentally. One has peeled a willow wand, woven it into a ring, and dropt it on my table. I could always tell if visitors had called in my absence, either by the bended twigs or grass, or the print of their shoes, and generally of what sex or age or quality they were by some slight trace left, as a flower dropt, or a bunch of grass plucked and thrown away, even as far off as the railroad, half a mile distant, or by the lingering odor of a cigar or pipe. Nay, I was frequently notified of the passage of a traveler along the highway sixty rods off by the scent of his pipe. . . .

I have never felt lonesome, or in the least opprest by a sense of solitude but once, and that was a few weeks after I came to the woods, when, for an hour, I doubted if the near neighborhood of man was not essential to a screne and healthy life. To be alone was something unpleasant. But I was at the same time conscious of a slight insanity in my mood, and seemed to foresee my

[4] From Chapter IV of "Walden."

recovery. In the midst of a gentle rain while these thoughts prevailed, I was suddenly sensible of such sweet and beneficent society in nature, in the very pattering of the drops, and in every sound and sight around my house, an infinite and unaccountable friendliness all at once like an atmosphere sustaining me, as made the fancied advantages of human neighborhood significant, and I have never thought of them since. Every little pine needle expanded and swelled with sympathy and befriended me. I was so distinctly made aware of the presence of something kindred to me, even in scenes which we are accustomed to call wild and dreary, and also that the nearest of blood to me and humanest was not a person nor a villager, that I thought no place could ever be strange to me again. . . .

I find it wholesome to be alone the greater part of the time. To be in company, even with the best, is soon wearisome and dissipating. I love to be alone. I never found the companion that was so companionable as solitude. We are for the most part more lonely when we go abroad among men than when we stay in our chambers. A man thinking or working is always alone, let him be where he will. Solitude is not measured by the miles of space that intervene between a man and his fellows. The really diligent student in one of the crowded hives of Cambridge College is as solitary as a dervish in the desert. The farmer can work alone in the field all day, hoeing or chopping, and not feel lonesome, because he is employed; but when he comes home at night he can not sit down in a room alone, at the mercy of his thoughts, but must be where he can "see the folks," and recreate, and, as he thinks, remunerate himself for his day's solitude; and hence he wonders how the student can sit alone in the house all night and most of the day without ennui and "the blues"; but he does not realize that the student, tho in the house, is still at work in his field, and chopping in his woods, as the farmer in his, and in turn seeks the same recreation and society that the latter does, tho it may be a more condensed form of it.

Society is commonly too cheap. We meet at very short intervals, not having had time to acquire any new value for each other. We meet at meals three times a day, and give each other a new taste of that old musty cheese that we are. We have to agree on a certain set of rules, called etiquette and politeness, to make this frequent meeting tolerable and that we need not come to open war. We meet at the post-office, and at the sociable, and about the fireside every night; we live thick and are in each other's way, and stumble over one another, and I think that we thus lose some respect for one another. Certainly less frequency would suffice for all important and hearty communications. Consider the girls in a factory—never alone, hardly in their dreams. It would be better if there were but one inhabitant to a square mile, as where I live. The value of a man is not in his skin, that we should touch him.

I have a great deal of company in my house; especially in the morning, when nobody calls. Let me suggest a few comparisons, that some one may convey an idea of my situation. I am no more lonely than the loon in the pond that laughs so loud, or than Walden pond itself. What company has that lonely lake, I pray? And yet it has not the blue devils, but the blue angels in it, in the azure tint of its waters. The sun is alone, except in thick weather, when there sometimes appear to be two, but one is a mock sun. God is alone—but the devil, he is far from being alone; he sees a great deal of company; he is legion. I am no more lonely than a single mullein or dandelion in a pasture, or a bean leaf, or sorrel, or a horse-fly, or a humble-bee. I am no more lonely than the Mill brook, or a weathercock, or the north star, or the south wind, or an April shower, or a January thaw, or the first spider in a new house.

I have occasional visits in the long winter evenings, when the snow falls fast and the wind howls in the wood, from an old settler and original proprietor, who is reported to have dug Walden pond, and stoned it, and fringed it with pine woods; who tells me stories of old time and of new eternity; and between us we manage to pass a cheerful evening, with social mirth and pleasant views of things, even without apples or cider; a most wise and humorous friend, whom I love much, who keeps himself more secret than ever did Goffe or Whalley; [5] and tho he is thought to be dead, none can show where he is buried. An elderly dame, too, dwells in my neighborhood, invisible to most persons, in whose odorous herb

[5] The English regicides who came to America, and after 1660 lived in concealment in New England, a part of the time in a cave near New Haven. William Goffe died in Hadley, Mass., in 1679. Edward Whalley, who had been one of Cromwell's major generals, died also in Hadley a year before Goffe.

garden I love to stroll sometimes, gathering simples and listening to her fables; for she has a genius of unequaled fertility, and her memory runs back farther than mythology, and she can tell me the original of every fable, and on what fact every one is founded, for the incidents occurred when she was young. A ruddy and lusty old dame, who delights in all weathers and seasons, and is likely to outlive all her children yet.

JAMES RUSSELL LOWELL

Born in 1819, died in 1891; graduated from Harvard in 1838; in 1855 became professor at Harvard; editor of *The Atlantic Monthly* in 1857-62, *The North American Review* in 1863-72; minister to Spain in 1877-80, and Great Britain in 1880-85; published "A Year's Life" in 1841, "The Vision of Sir Launfal" in 1845, "A Fable for Critics" in 1848, "The Biglow Papers" in 1848, and a second series in 1867, "Under the Willows" in 1868, "The Cathedral" in 1869; among his best-known prose works, "Conversations on Some of the Old Poets" published in 1845, "Fireside Travels" in 1864, "Among My Books" in 1870 and 1876, "My Study Windows" in 1871; his "Letters" edited by Charles Eliot Norton, published in 1893.

I

THE POET AS PROPHET [1]

POETS are the forerunners and prophets of changes in the moral world. Driven by their fine nature to search into and reverently contemplate the universal laws of the soul, they find some fragment of the broken tables of God's law, and interpret it, half-conscious of its mighty import. While philosophers are wrangling, and politicians playing at snapdragon with the des-

[1] From an essay contributed to *The Pioneer* in 1843. Lowell was the founder and editor of *The Pioneer*, Robert Carter being his associate. The magazine lived only three months. Charles Eliot Norton, the editor of Lowell's "Letters," says it "left its projectors burdened with a considerable debt." "I am deeply in debt," wrote Lowell afterward, when hesitating to undertake a journey, "and feel a twinge for every cent I spend."

tinies of millions, the poet, in the silent deeps of his soul, listens to those mysterious pulses which, from one central heart, send life and beauty through the finest veins of the universe, and utters truths to be sneered at, perchance, by contemporaries, but which become religion to posterity. Not unwisely ordered is that eternal destiny which renders the seer despised of men, since thereby he is but the more surely taught to lay his head meekly upon the mother-breast of Nature, and harken to the musical soft beating of her bounteous heart.

That Poesy, save as she can soar nearer to the blissful throne of the Supreme Beauty, is of no more use than all other beautiful things are, we are fain to grant. That she does not add to the outward wealth of the body, and that she is only so much more excellent than any bodily gift as spirit is more excellent than matter, we must also yield. But, inasmuch as all beautiful things are direct messages and revelations of himself, given us by our Father, and as Poesy is the searcher out and interpreter of all these, tracing by her inborn sympathy the invisible nerves which bind them harmoniously together, she is to be revered and cherished. The poet has a fresher memory of Eden, and of the path leading back thereto, than other men; so that we might almost deem him to have been conceived, at least, if not borne and nursed, beneath the ambrosial shadow of those dimly remembered bowers, and to have had his infant ears filled with the divine converse of angels, who then talked face to face with his sires, as with beloved younger brethren, and of whose golden words only the music remained to him, vibrating forever in his soul, and making him yearn to have all sounds of earth harmonize therewith. In the poet's lofty heart Truth hangs her aerie, and there Love flowers, scattering thence her winged seeds over all the earth with every wind of heaven. In all ages the poet's fiery words have goaded men to remember and regain their ancient freedom, and, when they had regained it, have tempered it with a love of beauty, so as that it should accord with the freedom of nature, and be as unmovably eternal as that. The dreams of poets are morning dreams, coming to them in the early dawn and daybreaking of great truths, and are surely fulfilled at last. They repeat them, as children do, and all Christendom, if it be not too busy with quarreling about the meaning of creeds, which have no meaning at all, listens with a shrug of the shoulders and a smile of pitying incredulity; for reformers are always madmen in their own age, and infallible saints in the next.

We love to go back to the writings of our old poets, for we find in them the tender germs of many a thought which now stands like a huge oak in the inward world, an ornament and a shelter. We can not help reading with awful interest what has been written or rudely scrawled upon the walls of this our earthly prison house, by former dwellers therein. From that which centuries have established, too, we may draw true principles of judgment for the poetry of our own day. A right knowledge and apprehension of the past teaches humbleness and self-sustainment to the present. Showing us what has been, it also reveals what can be done. Progress is Janus-faced, looking to the bygone as well as to the coming; and radicalism should not so much busy itself with lopping off the dead or seeming dead limbs, as with clearing away that poisonous rottenness around the roots, from which the tree has drawn the principle of death into its sap. A love of the beautiful and harmonious, which must be the guide and forerunner to every onward movement of humanity, is created and cherished more surely by pointing out what beauty dwells in anything, even the most deformed (for there is something in that also, else it could not even be), than by searching out and railing at all the foulnesses in nature.

Not till we have patiently studied beauty can we safely venture to look at defects, for not till then can we do it in that spirit of earnest love, which gives more than it takes away. Exultingly as we hail all signs of progress, we venerate the past also. The tendrils of the heart, like those of ivy, cling but the more closely to what they have clung to long, and even when that which they entwine crumbles beneath them, they still run greenly over the ruin, and beautify those defects which they can not hide. The past, as well as the present, molds the future, and the features of some remote progenitor will revive again freshly in the latest offspring of the womb of time. Our earth hangs well-nigh silent now, amid the chorus of her sister orbs, and not till past and present move harmoniously together will music once more vibrate on this long silent chord in the symphony of the universe.

II

THE FIRST OF THE MODERNS [2]

DRYDEN has now been in his grave nearly a hundred and seventy years; in the second class of English poets perhaps no one stands, on the whole, so high as he; during his lifetime, in spite of jealousy, detraction, unpopular politics, and a suspicious change of faith, his preeminence was conceded; he was the earliest complete type of the purely literary man, in the modern sense; there is a singular unanimity in allowing him a certain claim to greatness which would be denied to men as famous and more read—to Pope or Swift, for example; he is supposed, in some way or other, to have reformed English poetry. It is now about half a century since the only uniform edition of his works was edited by Scott. No library is complete without him, no name is more familiar than his, and yet it may be suspected that few writers are more thoroughly buried in that great cemetery of the "British Poets."

If contemporary reputation be often deceitful, posthumous fame may be generally trusted, for it is a verdict made up of the suffrages of the select men in succeeding generations. This verdict has been as good as unanimous in favor of Dryden. It is, perhaps, worth while to take a fresh observation of him, to consider him neither

[2] From the first essay in the first series entitled "Among My Books." Copyright, 1870, by James Russell Lowell. Published by Houghton, Mifflin Company.

as warning nor example, but to endeavor to make out what it is that has given so lofty and firm a position to one of the most unequal, inconsistent, and faulty writers that ever lived. He is a curious example of what we often remark of the living, but rarely of the dead—that they get credit for what they might be quite as much as for what they are—and posterity has applied to him one of his own rules of criticism, judging him by the best rather than the average of his achievement, a thing posterity is seldom wont to do. On the losing side in politics, it is true of his polemical writings as of Burke's—whom in many respects he resembles, and especially in that supreme quality of a reasoner, that his mind gathers not only heat, but clearness and expansion, by its own motion—that they have won his battle for him in the judgment of after times.

To us, looking back at him, he gradually becomes a singularly interesting and even picturesque figure. He is, in more senses than one, in language, in turn of thought, in style of mind, in the direction of his activity, the first of the moderns. He is the first literary man who was also a man of the world, as we understand the term. He succeeded Ben Jonson as the acknowledged dictator of wit and criticism, as Dr. Johnson, after nearly the same interval, succeeded him. All ages are, in some sense, ages of transition; but there are times when the transition is more marked, more rapid; and it is, perhaps, an ill fortune for a man of letters to arrive at maturity during such a period, still more to represent in himself the change that is going on, and to be an efficient cause in bringing it about. Unless, like Goethe, he is of a singularly uncontemporaneous nature, capable of being *tutta in se romita,* and of running parallel with his time rather than being sucked into its current, he will be thwarted in that harmonious development of native force which has so much to do with its steady and successful application. Dryden suffered, no doubt, in this way. Tho in creed he seems to have drifted backward in an eddy of the general current; yet of the intellectual movement of the time, so far certainly as literature shared in it, he could say, with Æneas, not only that he saw, but that himself was a great part of it.

That movement was, on the whole, a downward one, from faith to scepticism, from enthusiasm to cynicism, from the imagination to the understanding. It was in a direction altogether away from those springs of imagination and faith at which they of the last age had slaked the thirst or renewed the vigor of their souls. Dryden himself recognized that indefinable and gregarious influence which we call nowadays the spirit of the age, when he said that "every age has a kind of universal genius." He had also a just notion of that in which he lived; for he remarks, incidentally, that "all knowing ages are naturally sceptic and not at all bigoted, which, if I am not much deceived, is the proper character of our own." It may be conceived that he was even painfully half-aware of having fallen upon a time incapable, not merely of a great poet, but perhaps of any poet at all; for nothing is so sensitive to the chill of a skeptical atmosphere as that enthusiasm which, if it be not genius, is at least the beautiful illusion, that saves it from the baffling quibbles of self-consciousness. Thrice unhappy he who, born to see things as they might be, is schooled by circumstances to see them as people say they are—to read God in a prose translation. Such was Dryden's lot, and such, for a good part of his days, it was by his own choice. He who was of a stature to snatch the torch of life that flashes from lifted hand to hand along the generations, over the heads of inferior men, chose rather to be a link-boy to the stews. . . .

But at whatever period of his life we look at Dryden, and whatever, for the moment, may have been his poetic creed, there was something in the nature of the man that would not be wholly subdued to what it worked in. There are continual glimpses of something in him greater than he, hints of possibilities finer than anything he has done. You feel that the whole of him was better than any random specimens, tho of his best, seem to prove. *Incessu patet*, he has by times the large stride of the elder race, tho it sinks too often into the slouch of a man who has seen better days. His grand air may, in part, spring from a habit of easy superiority to his competitors; but must also, in part, be ascribed to an innate dignity of character. That this preeminence should have been so generally admitted, during his life, can only be explained by a bottom of good sense, kindliness, and sound judgment, whose solid worth could afford that many a flurry of vanity, petulance, and even error should flit across the surface and be forgotten. Whatever else Dryden may have been, the last and abiding impression of him is that he was thoroughly manly; and while it may be disputed whether he was a great poet, it may be said of him, as Wordsworth said of Burke, "that he was by far the greatest man of his age, not only abounding in knowledge himself, but feeding, in various directions, his most able contemporaries."

III

OF FAULTS FOUND IN SHAKESPEARE[3]

MR. MATTHEW ARNOLD seems to think that Shakespeare has damaged English poetry. I wish he had! It is true he lifted Dryden above himself in "All for Love"; but it was Dryden who said of him, by instinctive conviction rather than judgment, that within his magic circle none dared tread but he. Is he to blame for the extravagances of modern diction, which are but the reaction of the brazen age against the degeneracy of art into artifice, that has characterized the silver period in every literature? We see in them only the futile effort of misguided persons to torture out of language the secret of that inspiration which should be in themselves. We do not find the extravagances in Shakespeare himself. We never saw a line in any modern

[3] From the essay entitled "Shakespeare Once Again," printed in the first series entitled "Among My Books." Copyright, 1870, by James Russell Lowell. Published by Houghton, Mifflin Company.

poet that reminded us of him, and will venture to assert that it is only poets of the second class that find successful imitators. And the reason seems to us a very plain one. The genius of the great poet seeks repose in the expression of itself, and finds it at last in style, which is the establishment of a perfect mutual understanding between the worker and his material. The secondary intellect, on the other hand, seeks for excitement in expression, and stimulates itself into mannerism, which is the wilful obtrusion of self, as style is its unconscious abnegation. No poet of the first class has ever left a school, because his imagination is incommunicable; while, just as surely as the thermometer tells of the neighborhood of an iceberg, you may detect the presence of a genius of the second class in any generation by the influence of his mannerism, for that, being an artificial thing, is capable of reproduction. Dante, Shakespeare, Goethe, left no heirs either to the form or mode of their expression; while Milton, Sterne, and Wordsworth left behind them whole regiments uniformed with all their external characteristics.

We do not mean that great poetic geniuses may not have influenced thought (tho we think it would be difficult to show how Shakespeare had done so, directly and wilfully), but that they have not infected contemporaries or followers with mannerism. The quality in him which makes him at once so thoroughly English and so thoroughly cosmopolitan is that aeration of the understanding by the imagination which he has in common with all the greater poets, and which is the privilege of genius. The modern school,

which mistakes violence for intensity, seems to
catch its breath when it finds itself on the verge
of natural expression, and to say to itself, "Good
heavens! I had almost forgotten I was in-
spired!" But of Shakespeare we do not even
suspect that he ever remembered it. He does
not always speak in that intense way that flames
up in Lear and Macbeth through the rifts of a
soil volcanic with passion. He allows us here
and there the repose of a commonplace character,
the consoling distraction of a humorous one. He
knows how to be equable and grand without effort, so that we forget the altitude of thought
to which he has led us, because the slowly receding slope of a mountain stretching downward
by ample gradations gives a less startling impression of height than to look over the edge of
a ravine that makes but a wrinkle in its flank.

Shakespeare has been sometimes taxed with
the barbarism of profuseness and exaggeration.
But this is to measure him by a Sophoclean scale.
The simplicity of the antique tragedy is by no
means that of expression, but is of form merely.
In the utterance of great passions something
must be indulged to the extravagance of Nature;
the subdued tones to which pathos and sentiment
are limited can not express a tempest of the
soul. The range between the piteous "no more
but so," in which Ophelia compresses the heart-
break whose compression was to make her mad,
and that sublime appeal of Lear to the elements
of nature, only to be matched, if matched at all,
in the "Prometheus," is a wide one, and Shakespeare is as truly simple in the one as in the
other. The simplicity of poetry is not that of

prose, nor its clearness that of ready apprehension merely. To a subtile sense, a sense heightened by sympathy, those sudden fervors of phrase, gone ere one can say it lightens, that show us Macbeth groping among the complexities of thought in his conscience-clouded mind, and reveal the intricacy rather than enlighten it, while they leave the eye darkened to the literal meaning of the words, yet make their logical sequence the grandeur of the conception, and its truth to nature clearer than sober daylight could. There is an obscurity of mist rising from the undrained shallows of the mind, and there is the darkness of thunder-cloud gathering its electric masses with passionate intensity from the clear element of the imagination, not at random or wilfully, but by the natural processes of the creative faculty, to brood those flashes of expression that transcend rhetoric, and are only to be apprehended by the poetic instinct.

In that secondary office of imagination, where it serves the artist, not as the reason that shapes, but as the interpreter of his conceptions into words, there is a distinction to be noticed between the higher and lower mode in which it performs its function. It may be either creative or pictorial, may body forth the thought or merely image it forth. With Shakespeare, for example, imagination seems immanent in his very consciousness; with Milton, in his memory. In the one it sends, as if without knowing it, a fiery life into the verse,

"Sei die Braut das Wort,
    Bräutigam der Geist";

in the other it elaborates a certain pomp and elevation. Accordingly, the bias of the former is toward over-intensity, of the latter toward over-diffuseness. Shakespeare's temptation is to push a willing metaphor beyond its strength, to make a passion over-inform its tenement of words; Milton can not resist running a simile on into a fugue.

One always fancies Shakespeare in his best verses, and Milton at the keyboard of his organ. Shakespeare's language is no longer the mere vehicle of thought; it has become part of it, its very flesh and blood. The pleasure it gives us is unmixt, direct, like that from the smell of a flower or the flavor of a fruit. Milton sets everywhere his little pitfalls of bookish association for the memory. I know that Milton's manner is very grand. It is slow, it is stately, moving as in triumphal procession, with music, with historic banners, with spoils from every time and every region, and captive epithets, like huge Sicambrians, thrust their broad shoulders between us and the thought whose pomp they decorate. But it is manner, nevertheless, as is proved by the ease with which it is parodied, by the danger it is in of degenerating into mannerism whenever it forgets itself. Fancy a parody of Shakespeare—I do not mean of his words, but of his tone, for that is what distinguishes the master. You might as well try it with the Venus of Melos. In Shakespeare it is always the higher thing, the thought, the fancy, that is preeminent; it is Cæsar that draws all eyes, and not the chariot in which he rides, or the throng which is but the reverberation of his supremacy.

If not, how explain the charm with which he dominates in all tongues, even under the disenchantment of translation? Among the most alien races he is as solidly at home as a mountain seen from different sides by many lands, itself superbly solitary, yet the companion of all thoughts and domesticated in all imaginations.

IV

AMERICANS AS SUCCESSORS OF THE DUTCH [4]

For more than a century the Dutch were the laughing-stock of polite Europe. They were butter-firkins, swillers of beer and schnapps, and their *vrouws* from whom Holbein painted the all but loveliest of Madonnas, Rembrandt the graceful girl who sits immortal on his knee in Dresden, and Rubens his abounding goddesses, were the synonyms of clumsy vulgarity. Even so late as Irving the ships of the greatest navigators in the world were represented as sailing equally well stern-foremost. That the aristocratic Venetians should have

> "Riveted with gigantic piles
> Thorough the center their new catchèd miles"

was heroic. But the far more marvelous achieve-

[4] From the essay entitled "On a Certain Condescension in Foreigners," printed in "From My Study Windows." Copyright, 1870, 1871, 1890, by James Russell Lowell. Published by Houghton, Mifflin Company.

ment of the Dutch in the same kind was ludicrous even to republican Marvell. Meanwhile, during that very century of scorn, they were the best artists, sailors, merchants, bankers, printers, scholars, jurisconsults, and statesmen in Europe, and the genius of Motley has revealed them to us, earning a right to themselves by the most heroic struggle in human annals. But, alas! they were not merely simple burghers who had fairly made themselves High Mightinesses, and could treat on equal terms with anointed kings, but their commonwealth carried in its bosom the germs of democracy. They even unmuzzled, at least after dark, that dreadful mastiff, the Press, whose scent is, or ought to be, so keen for wolves in sheep's clothing and for certain other animals in lions' skins. They made fun of sacred majesty, and, what was worse, managed uncommonly well without it. In an age when periwigs made so large a part of the natural dignity of man people with such a turn of mind were dangerous. How could they seem other than vulgar and hateful?

In the natural course of things we succeeded to this unenviable position of general butt. The Dutch had thriven under it pretty well, and there was hope that we could at least contrive to worry along. And we certainly did in a very redoubtable fashion. Perhaps we deserved some of the sarcasm more than our Dutch predecessors in office. We had nothing to boast of in arts or letters, and were given to bragging overmuch of our merely material prosperity, due quite as much to the virtue of our continent as to our own. There was some truth in Carlyle's sneer

after all. Till we had succeeded in some higher
way than this, we had only the success of physical growth. Our greatness, like that of enormous
Russia, was greatness on the map—barbarian
mass only; but had we gone down, like that other
Atlantis, in some vast cataclysm, we should have
covered but a pin's point on the chart of memory, compared with those ideal spaces occupied
by tiny Attica and cramped England. At the
same time, our critics somewhat too easily forgot
that material must make ready the foundation
for ideal triumphs, that the arts have no chance
in poor countries. But it must be allowed that
democracy stood for a great deal in our short-
coming. The *Edinburgh Review* never would
have thought of asking, "Who reads a Russian
book?" and England was satisfied with iron from
Sweden without being impertinently inquisitive
after her painters and statuaries. Was it that
they expected too much from the mere miracle
of freedom? Is it not the highest art of a republic
to make men of flesh and blood, and not the
marble ideals of such? It may be fairly doubted
whether we have produced this higher type of
man yet. Perhaps it is the collective, not the
individual humanity that is to have a chance of
nobler development among us. We shall see. We
have a vast amount of imported ignorance, and,
still worse, of native ready-made knowledge, to
digest before even the preliminaries of such a
consummation can be arranged. We have got to
learn that statesmanship is the most complicated
of all arts, and to come back to the apprenticeship
system too hastily abandoned. . . .

So long as we continue to be the most common-schooled and the least cultivated people in the world, I suppose we must consent to endure this condescending manner of foreigners toward us. The more friendly they mean to be the more ludicrously prominent it becomes. They can never appreciate the immense amount of silent work that has been done here, making this continent slowly fit for the abode of man, and which will demonstrate itself, let us hope, in the character of the people. Outsiders can only be expected to judge a nation by the amount it has contributed to the civilization of the world; the amount, that is, that can be seen and handled. A great place in history can only be achieved by competitive examinations, nay, by a long course of them. How much new thought have we contributed to the common stock? Till that question can be triumphantly answered, or needs no answer, we must continue to be simply interesting as an experiment, to be studied as a problem, and not respected as an attained result or an accomplished solution. Perhaps, as I have hinted, their patronizing manner toward us is the fair result of their failing to see here anything more than a poor imitation, a plaster-cast of Europe.

Are they not partly right? If the tone of the uncultivated American has too often the arrogance of the barbarian, is not that of the cultivated as often vulgarly apologetic? In the America they meet with is there the simplicity, the manliness, the absence of sham, the faith in human nature, the sensitiveness to duty and implied obligation, that in any way distinguishes us from what our orators call "the effete civilization of the Old World"? Is there a politician among us daring enough (except a Dana[5] here and there) to risk his future on the chance of our keeping our word with the exactness of superstitious communities like England? Is it certain that we shall be ashamed of a bankruptcy of honor, if we can only keep the letter of our bond? I hope we shall be able to answer all these questions with a frank yes.

At any rate, we would advise our visitors that we are not merely curious creatures, but belong to the family of man, and that, as individuals, we are not to be always subjected to the competitive examination above mentioned, even if we acknowledged their competence as an examining board. Above all, we beg them to remember that America is not to us, as to them, a mere object of external interest to be discust and analyzed, but in us, part of our very marrow. Let them not suppose that we conceive of ourselves as exiles from the graces and amenities of an older date than we, tho very much at home in a state of things not yet all it might be or should be, but which we mean to make so, and which we find both wholesome and pleasant for men (tho perhaps not for *dilettanti*) to live in. ''The full tide of human existence''[6] may be felt here as keenly as Johnson felt it at Charing Cross, and in a larger sense. I know one person who

[5] The reference is to Richard Henry Dana, author of "Two Years Before the Mast," who in 1876 was appointed by President Grant minister to England, but failed of confirmation in the Senate, owing to political intrigues due to his independence. Lowell appears to have inserted this reference to Dana in an edition published subsequent to the first, the date of the first being 1871.

[6] A remark of Dr. Johnson's as reported by Boswell.

is singular enough to think Cambridge the very
best spot on the habitable globe. ''Doubtless
God could have made a better, but doubtless He
never did.''

It will take England a great while to get over
her airs of patronage toward us, or even passably
to conceal them. She can not help confounding
the people with the country, and regarding us
as lusty juveniles. She has a conviction that
whatever good there is in us is wholly English,
when the truth is that we are worth nothing
except so far as we have disinfected ourselves
of Anglicism. She is especially condescending
just now, and lavishes sugar-plums on us as if
we had not outgrown them. I am no believer in
sudden conversions, especially in sudden conversions to a favorable opinion of people who have
just proved you to be mistaken in judgment and
therefore unwise in policy. I never blamed her
for not wishing well to democracy—how should
she?—but *Alabamas* are not wishes. Let her not
be too hasty in believing Mr. Reverdy Johnson's [7]
pleasant words. Tho there is no thoughtful man
in America who would not consider a war with
England the greatest of calamities, yet the feeling toward her here is very far from cordial,
whatever our minister may say in the effusion
that comes after ample dining. Mr. Adams, [8]

[7] Reverdy Johnson of Maryland, Mr. Adams's successor
as minister to England, negotiated a settlement of the
Alabama dispute, which was unfavorably received in this
country and finally rejected by the Senate, which led to his
recall in 1869.

[8] Charles Francis Adams, our minister to England from
1861 to 1867, made this remark to a British cabinet minister at the time of the threatened sailing of the Laird rams.

with his famous "My Lord, this means war," perfectly represented his country. Justly or not, we have a feeling that we have been wronged, not merely insulted. The only sure way of bringing about a healthy relation between the two countries is for Englishmen to clear their minds of the notion that we are always to be treated as a kind of inferior and deported Englishman whose nature they perfectly understand, and whose back they accordingly stroke the wrong way of the fur with amazing perseverance. Let them learn to treat us naturally on our merits as human beings, as they would a German or a Frenchman, and not as if we were a kind of counterfeit Briton whose crime appeared in every shade of difference, and before long there would come that right feeling which we naturally call a good understanding. The common blood, and still more the common language, are fatal instruments of misapprehension. Let them give up trying to understand us, still more thinking that they do, and acting in various absurd ways as the necessary consequence, for they will never arrive at that devoutly-to-be-wished consummation till they learn to look at us as we are and not as they suppose us to be. Dear old long-estranged mother-in-law, it is a great many years since we parted. Since 1660, when you married again, you have been a step-mother to us. Put on your spectacles, dear madam. Yes, we have grown, and changed likewise. You would not let us darken your doors, if you could possibly help it.

We know that perfectly well. But pray, when we look to be treated as men, don't shake that rattle in our faces, nor talk baby to us any longer.

"Do, child, go to it grandam, child;
Give grandam kingdom, and it grandam will
Give it a plum, a cherry, and a fig!"

CHARLES A. DANA

Born in 1819, died in 1897; joined the Brook Farm Community in 1842; an editor of the New York *Tribune* in 1847-62; Assistant Secretary of War in 1863-64; became editor of the New York *Sun* in 1868, remaining editor until his death; published "A Household Book of Poetry" in 1857; joint editor with George Ripley of the "American Encyclopedia."

GREELEY AS A MAN OF GENIUS[1]

THOSE who have examined the history of this remarkable man and who know how to estimate the friendlessness, the disabilities, and the disadvantages which surrounded his childhood and youth; the scanty opportunities, or rather the absence of all opportunity, of education; the destitution and loneliness amid which he struggled for the possession of knowledge; and the unflinching zeal and pertinacity with which he provided for himself the materials for intellectual growth, will heartily echo the popular judgment that he was indeed a man of genius, marked out from his cradle to inspire, animate, and instruct others.

From the first, when a child in his father's log cabin, lying upon the hearth that he might read by the flickering firelight, his attention was given almost exclusively to public and political affairs. This determined his vocation as a

---

[1] From an article printed in the New York *Sun*, December 5, 1872. Greeley had died November 29, of this year.

journalist; and he seems never to have felt any attraction toward any other of the intellectual professions. He never had a thought of being a physician, a clergyman, an engineer, or a lawyer. Private questions, individual controversies had little concern for him except as they were connected with public interests. Politics and newspapers were his delight, and he learned to be a printer in order that he might become a newspaper maker. And after he was the editor of a newspaper, what chiefly engaged him was the discussion of political and social questions. His whole greatness as a journalist was in this sphere. For the collection and digestion of news, with the exception of election statistics, he had no great fondness and no special ability. He valued talent in that department only because he knew it was essential to the success of the newspaper he loved. His own thoughts were always elsewhere.

Accordingly there have been journalists who as such, strictly speaking, have surpassed him. Minds not devoted to particular doctrines, not absorbed in the advocacy of cherished ideas—in a word, minds, that believe little and aim only at the passing success of a day—may easily excel one like him in the preparation of a mere newspaper. Mr. Greeley was the antipodes of all such persons. He was always absolutely in earnest. His convictions were intense; he had that peculiar courage, most precious in a great man, which enables him to adhere to his own line of action despite the excited appeals of friends and the menaces of variable public opinion; and his constant purpose was to assert his principles, to fight for them, and present them to the public in the way most likely to give them the same hold upon other minds which they had upon his own. In fact, he was not so much a journalist, in the proper meaning of that term, as a pamphleteer or writer of leading articles.

In this sphere of effort he had scarcely an equal. His command of language was extraordinary, tho he had little imagination and his vocabulary was limited; but he possest the faculty of expressing himself in a racy, virile manner, within the apprehension of every reader. As he treated every topic in a practical rather than a philosophical spirit, and with strong feeling rather than infallible logic, so he never wrote above the heads of the public. What he said was plain, clear, striking. His illustrations were quaint and homely, sometimes even vulgar, but they never failed to tell. He was gifted also with an excellent humor which greatly enlivened his writing. In retort, especially when provoked, he was dangerous to his antagonist; and tho his reasoning might be faulty, he would frequently gain his cause by a flash of wit that took the public, and, as it were, hustled his adversary out of court. But he was not always a victorious polemic. His vehemence in controversy was sometimes too precipitate for his prudence; he would rush into a fight with his armor unfastened, and with only a part of the necessary weapons; and as the late Washington Hunt [2] once exprest it, he could be more damaging to his friends than to his opponents. . . .

[2] Governor of New York in 1851-53, having been elected by the Whigs.

The occasional uncertainty of his judgment was probably due, in a measure, to the deficiency of his education. Self-educated men are not always endowed with the strong logical faculty and sure good sense which are developed and strengthened by thorough intellectual culture. Besides, a man of powerful intellect who is not regularly disciplined is apt to fall into an exaggerated mental self-esteem from which more accurate training and information would have preserved him. But the very imperfection of Greeley's early studies had a compensation in the fact that they left him, in all the tendencies and habits of his mind, an American. No foreign mixture of thought or tradition went to the composition of his strong intelligence. Of all the great men who have become renowned on this side of the Atlantic he was most purely and entirely the product of the country and its institutions. Accordingly, a sturdy reliance on his own conclusions and a readiness to defy the world in their behalf were among his most strongly marked characteristics.

But a kind of moral unsteadiness diminished his power. The miseries of his childhood had left their trace in a querulous, lamentable, helpless tone of feeling, into which he fell upon any little misfortune or disappointment; and as he grew older he came to lack hope.

JAMES PARTON

Born in 1822, died in 1891; noted biographer and miscellaneous writer; published "Life of Horace Greeley" in 1855, "Aaron Burr" in 1857, "Andrew Jackson" in 1860, "Benjamin Franklin" in 1864, "Thomas Jefferson" in 1874, "Voltaire" in 1881; author of several other books.

AARON BURR AND MADAME JUMEL[1]

IN the year 1822 M. Jumel lost a considerable part of his fortune, and madame returned alone to New York, bringing with her a prodigious quantity of grand furniture and paintings. Retiring to a seat in the upper part of Manhattan Island, which she possest in her own right,[2] she began with native energy the task of restoring her husband's broken fortunes. She cultivated her farm; she looked vigilantly to the remains of the estate; she economized. In 1828, when M. Jumel returned to the United States, they were not as rich as in former days, but their estate was ample for all rational purposes and enjoyments. In 1832 M. Jumel, a man of mag-

---

[1] From the "Life of Burr."

[2] Still standing on an eminence near High Bridge and popularly known as the Jumel House, tho it would more properly be called the Morris House. It was built by Col. Roger Morris of the British army after the old French war, his wife being Mary Philipse, of Philipse Manor, a former sweetheart of Washington. During Washington's sojourn in New York in 1776 it became his headquarters. It is now owned by New York City and has become a museum of historical relics.

nificent proportions, very handsome, and perfectly preserved (a great waltzer at seventy), was thrown from a wagon and fatally injured. He died in a few days. Madame was then little past her prime.

There was talk of cholera in the city. Madame Jumel resolved upon taking a carriage tour in the country. Before setting out she wished to take legal advice respecting some real estate, and as Colonel Burr's reputation in that department was preeminent, to his office in Reade street she drove. In other days he had known her well, and tho many an eventful year had passed since he had seen her, he recognized her at once. He received her in his courtliest manner, complimented her with admirable tact, listened with soft deference to her statement. He was the ideal man of business—confidential, self-possest, polite—giving his client the flattering impression that the faculties of his whole soul were concentrated upon the affair in hand. She was charmed, yet feared him. He took the papers, named the day when his opinion would be ready, and handed her to her carriage with winning grace. At seventy-eight years of age, he was still straight, active, agile, fascinating.

On the appointed day she sent to his office a relative, a student of law, to receive his opinion. This young gentleman, timid and inexperienced, had an immense opinion of Burr's talents; had heard all good and all evil of him; supposed him to be, at least, the acutest of possible men. He went. Burr behaved to him in a manner so exquisitely pleasing that, to this hour, he has the liveliest recollection of the scene. No topic was introduced but such as were familiar and interesting to young men. His manners were such as this age of slangy familiarity can not so much as imagine. The young gentleman went home to Madame Jumel only to extol and glorify him.

Madame and her party began their journey, revisiting Ballston, whither, in former times, she had been wont to go in a chariot drawn by eight horses; visiting Saratoga, then in the beginning of its celebrity, where, in exactly ten minutes after her arrival, the decisive lady bought a house and all it contained. Returning to New York to find that her mansion had been despoiled by robbers in her absence, she lived for a while in the city. Colonel Burr called upon the young gentleman who had been madame's messenger, and, after their acquaintance had ripened, said to him, "Come into my office; I can teach you more in a year than you can learn in ten in an ordinary way." The proposition being submitted to Madame Jumel, she, anxious for the young man's advancement, gladly and gratefully consented. He entered the office. Burr kept him close at his books. He did teach him more in a year than he could have learned in ten in an ordinary way. Burr lived then in Jersey City. His office (23 Nassau street) swarmed with applicants for aid, and he seemed now to have quite lost the power of refusing. In no other respects, bodily or mental, did he exhibit signs of decrepitude.

Some months passed on without his again meeting Madame Jumel. At the suggestion of the student, who felt exceedingly grateful to Burr for the solicitude with which he assisted in his studies, Madame Jumel invited Colonel Burr to dinner. It was a grand banquet, at which he displayed all the charms of his manner, and shone to conspicuous advantage. On handing to dinner the giver of the feast, he said: "I give you my hand, madame; my heart has long been yours." This was supposed to be merely a compliment, and was little remarked at the time. Colonel Burr called upon the lady; called frequently; became ever warmer in his attentions; proposed, at length, and was refused. He still plied his suit, however, and obtained at last, not the lady's consent, but an undecided No. Improving his advantage on the instant, he said, in a jocular manner, that he should bring out a clergyman to Fort Washington on a certain day, and there he would once more solicit her hand.

He was as good as his word. At the time appointed, he drove out in his gig to the lady's country residence, accompanied by Dr. Bogart, the very clergyman who, just fifty years before, had married him to the mother of his Theodosia. The lady was embarrassed, and still refused. But then the scandal! And, after all, why not? Her estate needed a vigilant guardian, and the old house was lonely. After much hesitation, she at length consented to be drest, and to receive her visitors. And she was married. The ceremony was witnessed only by the members of Madame Jumel's family, and by the eight servants of the household, who peered eagerly in at the doors and windows. The ceremony over, Mrs. Burr ordered supper. Some bins of

M. Jumel's wine-cellar, that had not been opened for half a century, were laid under contribution. The little party was a very merry one. The parson, in particular, it is remembered, was in the highest spirits, overflowing with humor and anecdote. Except for Colonel Burr's great age (which was not apparent), the match seemed not an unwise one. The lurking fear he had had of being a poor and homeless old man was put to rest. She had a companion who had been ever agreeable, and her estate a steward than whom no one living was supposed to be more competent.

As a remarkable circumstance connected with this marriage, it may be just mentioned that there was a woman in New York who had aspired to the hand of Colonel Burr, and who, when she heard of his union with another, wrung her hands and shed tears! A feeling of that nature can seldom, since the creation of man, have been excited by the marriage of a man on the verge of fourscore.

A few days after the wedding the "happy pair" paid a visit to Connecticut, of which State a nephew of Colonel Burr was then governor. They were received with attention. At Hartford Burr advised his wife to sell out her shares in the bridge over the Connecticut at that place, and invest the proceeds in real estate. She ordered them sold. The stock was in demand, and the shares brought several thousand dollars. The purchasers offered to pay her the money, but she said, "No; pay it to my husband." To him, accordingly, it was paid, and he had it sewed up in his pocket, a prodigious bulk, and brought it to New York, and deposited it in his own bank, to his own credit.

Texas was then beginning to attract the tide of emigration which, a few years later, set so strongly thither. Burr had always taken a great interest in that country. Persons with whom he had been variously connected in life had a scheme on foot for settling a large colony of Germans on a tract of land in Texas. A brig had been chartered, and the project was in a state of forwardness, when the possession of a sum of money enabled Burr to buy shares in the enterprise. The greater part of the money which he had brought from Hartford was invested in this way. It proved a total loss. The time had not yet come for emigration to Texas. The Germans became discouraged and separated, and, to complete the failure of the scheme, the title of the lands in the confusion of the times proved defective. Meanwhile madame, who was a remarkably thrifty woman, with a talent for the management of property, wondered that her husband made no allusion to the subject of the investment; for the Texas speculation had not been mentioned to her. She caused him to be questioned on the subject. He begged to intimate to the lady's messenger that it was no affair of hers, and requested him to remind the lady that she now had a husband to manage her affairs, and one who would manage them.

Coolness between the husband and wife was the result of this colloquy. Then came remonstrances. Then estrangement. Burr got into the habit of remaining at his office in the city. Then partial reconciliation. Full of schemes and speculations to the last, without retaining any of his former ability to operate successfully, he lost more money, and more, and more. The patience of the lady was exhausted. She filed a complaint accusing him of infidelity, and praying that he might have no more control or authority over her affairs. The accusation is now known to have been groundless; nor, indeed, at the time was it seriously believed. It was used merely as the most convenient legal mode of depriving him of control over her property. At first he answered the complaint vigorously, but afterward he allowed it to go by default, and proceedings were carried no further. A few short weeks of happiness, followed by a few months of alternate estrangement and reconciliation, and this union, that began not inauspiciously, was, in effect, tho never in law, dissolved. What is strangest of all is that the lady, tho she never saw her husband during the last two years of his life, cherished no ill-will toward him, and shed tears at his death. To this hour Madame Jumel thinks and speaks of him with kindness, attributing what was wrong or unwise in his conduct to the infirmities of age.

Men of seventy-eight have been married before and since. But, probably, never has there been another instance of a man of that age winning a lady of fortune and distinction, grieving another by his marriage, and exciting suspicions of incontinence against himself by his attentions to a third!

FRANCIS PARKMAN

Born in 1823, died in 1893; graduated from Harvard in
1844; studied law, but abandoned it for literature; his
eyesight so defective he was nearly blind; professor at
Harvard in 1871-72; published his "Conspiracy of Pontiac"
in 1851, "Pioneers of France in the New World" in 1865,
"Jesuits in North America" in 1867, "La Salle and the
Discovery of the Great West" in 1869, "The Old Régime in
Canada" in 1874, "Count Frontenac" in 1877, "Montcalm
and Wolfe" in 1884, "A Half-Century of Conflict" in 1892.

I

CHAMPLAIN'S BATTLE WITH THE IROQUOIS [1]
(1609)

IT was ten o'clock in the evening when, near
a projecting point of land, which was probably
Ticonderoga, they descried dark objects in motion on the lake before them. These were a

---

[1] From Chapter X of "The Pioneers of France in the
New World." Copyright, 1865, by Francis Parkman. Published by Little, Brown & Co. It may be noted here that one
of the most remarkable coincidences in the history of ex-
ploration is the fact that, at the time of this battle between
Champlain and the Iroquois, Henry Hudson was ascending
the river that bears his name. Hudson went as far as the
site of Albany. The two explorers, therefore, at the same
time had reached points distant from each other only about one
hundred miles, and yet each was unaware of the other's
presence. Champlain and Hudson represented the opposing
forces in race and system of government which, from that
time until the death of Montcalm at Quebec, were to contend
for mastery of the North American continent.

flotilla of Iroquois canoes, heavier and slower than theirs, for they were made of oak bark. Each party saw the other, and the mingled war-cries pealed over the darkened water. The Iroquois, who were near the shore, having no stomach for an aquatic battle, landed, and, making night hideous with their clamors, began to barricade themselves. Champlain could see them in the woods, laboring like beavers, hacking down trees with iron axes taken from the Canadian tribes in war, and with stone hatchets of their own making. The allies remained on the lake, a bowshot from the hostile barricade, their canoes made fast together by poles lasht across. All night they danced with as much vigor as the frailty of their vessels would permit, their throats making amends for the enforced restraint of their limbs. It was agreed on both sides that the fight should be deferred till daybreak; but meanwhile a commerce of abuse, sarcasm, menace, and boasting gave unceasing exercise to the lungs and fancy of the combatants—"much," says Champlain, "like the besiegers and besieged in a beleaguered town."

As day approached, he and his two followers put on the light armor of the time. Champlain wore the doublet and long hose then in vogue. Over the doublet he buckled on a breastplate, and probably a back-piece, while his thighs were protected by cuisses of steel, and his head by a plumed casque. Across his shoulder hung the strap of his bandoleer, or ammunition-box; at his side was his sword, and in his hand his arquebus. Such was the equipment of this ancient Indian-fighter, whose exploits date eleven years before the landing of the Puritans at Plymouth, and sixty-six years before King Philip's War.

Each of the three Frenchmen was in a separate canoe, and, as it grew light, they kept themselves hidden, either by lying at the bottom, or covering themselves with an Indian robe. The canoes approached the shore, and all landed without opposition at some distance from the Iroquois, whom they presently could see filing out of their barricade, tall, strong men, some two hundred in number, the boldest and fiercest warriors of North America. They advanced through the forest with a steadiness which excited the admiration of Champlain. Among them could be seen three chiefs, made conspicuous by their tall plumes. Some bore shields of wood and hide, and some were covered with a kind of armor made of tough twigs interlaced with a vegetable fiber supposed by Champlain to be cotton.

The allies, growing anxious, called with loud cries for their champion, and opened their ranks that he might pass to the front. He did so, and, advancing before his red companions in arms, stood revealed to the gaze of the Iroquois, who, beholding the warlike apparition in their path, stared in mute amazement. "I looked at them," says Champlain, "and they looked at me. When I saw them getting ready to shoot their arrows at us, I leveled my arquebus, which I had loaded with four balls, and aimed straight at one of the three chiefs. The shot brought down two, and wounded another. On this, our Indians set up such a yelling that one could not have heard a thunder-clap, and all the while the arrows flew thick on both sides. The Iroquois were greatly astonished and frightened to see two of their men killed so quickly, in spite of their arrow-proof armor. As I was reloading, one of my companions fired a shot from the woods, which so increased their astonishment that, seeing their chiefs dead, they abandoned the field and fled into the depth of the forest." The allies dashed after them. Some of the Iroquois were killed, and more were taken. Camp, canoes, provisions, all were abandoned, and many weapons flung down in the panic flight. The victory was complete.

At night the victors led out one of the prisoners, told him that he was to die by fire, and ordered him to sing his death-song, if he dared. Then they began the torture, and presently scalped their victim alive, when Champlain, sickening at the sight, begged leave to shoot him. They refused, and he turned away in anger and disgust; on which they called him back and told him to do as he pleased. He turned again and a shot from his arquebus put the wretch out of misery.

The scene filled him with horror; but, a few months later, on the Place de la Grève at Paris, he might have witnessed tortures equally revolting and equally vindictive, inflicted on the regicide Ravaillac[2] by the sentence of grave and learned judges.

---

[2] Ravaillac, a religious fanatic, was the assassin of Henry IV of France. After climbing on to the rear of the King's carriage in one of the streets of Paris, he stabbed the King twice, the second wound proving fatal. Ravaillac met his death by being torn asunder by horses.

II

THE DEATH OF LA SALLE [3]
(1687)

NIGHT came; the woods grew dark; the evening meal was finished, and the evening pipes were smoked. The order of the guard was arranged; and, doubtless by design, the first hour of the night was assigned to Moranget, the second to Saget, and the third to Nika. Gun in hand, each stood watch in turn over the silent but not sleeping forms around him, till, his time expiring, he called the man who was to relieve him, wrapt himself in his blanket, and was soon buried in a slumber that was to be his last. Now the assassins rose. Duhaut and Hiens stood with their guns cocked, ready to shoot down any one of the destined victims who should resist or fly. The surgeon, with an ax, stole toward the three sleepers, and struck a rapid blow at each in turn. Saget and Nika died with little movement; but Moranget started spasmodically into a sitting posture, gasping and unable to speak; and the murderers compelled De Marle,

[3] From Chapter XXVII of "La Salle and the Discovery of the Great West." La Salle was assassinated by some of his own men, near a branch of the Trinity river in Texas. He had sailed from France in 1684 for the purpose of founding a colony at the mouth of the Mississippi, and had landed at Metagorda Bay, mistaking it for an outlet of the Mississippi. He was about to sail for Canada in order to get supplies for his colony, when he met the fate here described. Copyright, 1860, 1879, 1897, by Francis Parkman, published by Little, Brown & Company.

who was not in their plot, to compromise himself
by dispatching him.

The floodgates of murder were open, and the
torrent must have its way. Vengeance and safety alike demanded the death of La Salle. Hiens,
or "English Jem," alone seems to have hesitated; for he was one of those to whom that
stern commander had always been partial. Meanwhile, the intended victim was still at his camp,
about six miles distant. It is easy to picture,
with sufficient accuracy, the features of the scene
—the sheds of bark and branches, beneath which,
among blankets and buffalo-robes, camp utensils,
pack-saddles, rude harness, guns, powder-horns,
and bullet-pouches, the men lounged away the
hour, sleeping or smoking, or talking among
themselves; the blackened kettles that hung from
tripods of poles over the fires; the Indians strolling about the place or lying, like dogs in the
sun, with eyes half-shut, yet all observant; and,
in the neighboring meadow, the horses grazing
under the eye of a watchman.

It was the eighteenth of March. Moranget
and his companions had been expected to return
the night before; but the whole day passed, and
they did not appear. La Salle became very
anxious. He resolved to go and look for them;
but, not well knowing the way, he told the Indians who were about the camp that he would
give them a hatchet if they would guide him.
One of them accepted the offer; and La Salle
prepared to set out in the morning, at the same
time directing Joutel to be ready to go with
him. Joutel says: "That evening, while we
were talking about what could have happened

to the absent men, he seemed to have a presentiment of what was to take place. He asked me if I had heard of any machinations against them, or if I had noticed any bad design on the part of Duhaut and the rest. I answered that I had heard nothing, except that they sometimes complained of being found fault with so often; and that this was all I knew, besides which, as they were persuaded that I was in his interest, they would not have told me of any bad design they might have. We were very uneasy all the rest of the evening.''

In the morning La Salle set out with his Indian guide. He had changed his mind with regard to Joutel, whom he now directed to remain in charge of the camp and to keep a careful watch. He told the friar Anastase Douay to come with him instead of Joutel, whose gun, which was the best in the party, he borrowed for the occasion, as well as his pistol. The three proceeded on their way—La Salle, the friar, and the Indian. "All the way," writes the friar, "he spoke to me of nothing but matters of piety, grace, and predestination; enlarging on the debt he owed to God, who had saved him from so many perils during more than twenty years of travel in America. Suddenly, I saw him overwhelmed with a profound sadness, for which he himself could not account. He was so much moved that I scarcely knew him." He soon recovered his usual calmness; and they walked on till they approached the camp of Duhaut, which was on the farther side of a small river. Looking about him with the eye of a woodsman, La Salle saw two eagles circling in the air nearly over him, as if attracted by carcasses of beasts or men. He fired his gun and his pistol, as a summons to any of his followers who might be within hearing. The shots reached the ears of the conspirators.

Rightly conjecturing by whom they were fired, several of them, led by Duhaut, crossed the river at a little distance above, where trees or other intervening objects hid them from sight. Duhaut and the surgeon crouched like Indians in the long, dry, reed-like grass of the last summer's growth, while L'Archeveque stood in sight near the bank. La Salle, continuing to advance, soon saw him, and calling to him, demanded where was Moranget. The man, without lifting his hat, or any show of respect, replied in an agitated and broken voice, but with a tone of studied insolence, that Moranget was strolling about somewhere. La Salle rebuked and menaced him. He rejoined with increased insolence, drawing back, as he spoke, toward the ambuscade, while the incensed commander advanced to chastise him. At that moment, a shot was fired from the grass, instantly followed by another; and, pierced through the brain, La Salle dropt dead.

The friar at his side stood terror-stricken, unable to advance or to fly; when Duhaut, rising from the ambuscade, called out to him to take courage, for he had nothing to fear. The murderers now came forward, and with wild looks gathered about their victim. "There thou liest, great Bashaw! There thou liest!" exclaimed the surgeon Liotot, in base exultation over the unconscious corpse. With mockery and insult, they stript it naked, dragged it into the bushes, and left it there, a prey to buzzards and wolves.

Thus, in the vigor of his manhood, at the age of forty-three, died Robert Cavelier de La Salle, "one of the greatest men," writes Tonty, "of this age"; without question one of the most remarkable explorers whose names live in history. His faithful officer Joutel thus sketches his portrait: "His firmness, his courage, his great knowledge of the arts and sciences, which made him equal to every undertaking, and his untiring energy, which enabled him to surmount every obstacle, would have won at last a glorious success for his grand enterprise, had not all his fine qualities been counterbalanced by a haughtiness of manner which often made him unsupportable, and by a harshness toward those under his command which drew upon him an implacable hatred, and was at last the cause of his death."

The enthusiasm of the disinterested and chivalrous Champlain was not the enthusiasm of La Salle, nor had he any part in the self-devoted zeal of the early Jesuit explorers. He belonged not to the age of the knight-errant and the saint, but to the modern world of practical study and practical action. He was the hero, not of a principle nor of a faith, but simply of a fixt idea and a determined purpose. As often happens with concentered and energetic natures, his purpose was to him a passion and an inspiration; and he clung to it with a certain fanaticism of devotion. It was the offspring of an ambition vast and comprehensive, yet acting in the interest both of France and of civilization.

Serious in all things, incapable of the lighter pleasures, incapable of repose, finding no joy but in the pursuit of great designs, too shy for society and too reserved for popularity, often unsympathetic and always seeming so, smothering emotions which he could not utter, schooled to universal distrust, stern to his followers and pitiless to himself, bearing the brunt of every hardship and every danger, demanding of others an equal constancy joined to an implicit deference, heeding no counsel but his own, attempting the impossible and grasping at what was too vast to hold—he contained in his own complex and painful nature the chief springs of his triumphs, his failures, and his death.

It is easy to reckon up his defects, but it is not easy to hide from sight the Roman virtues that redeemed them. Beset by a throng of enemies, he stands, like the King of Israel, head and shoulders above them all. He was a tower of adamant, against whose impregnable front hardship and danger, the rage of man and of the elements, the southern sun, the northern blast, fatigue, famine, and disease, delay, disappointment, and deferred hope emptied their quivers in vain. That very pride which, Coriolanus-like, declared itself most sternly in the thickest press of foes, has in it something to challenge admiration. Never, under the impenetrable mail of paladin or crusader, beat a heart of more intrepid mettle than within the stoic panoply that armed the breast of La Salle. To estimate aright the marvels of his patient fortitude, one must follow on his track through the vast scene of his interminable journeyings, those thousands of weary miles of forest, marsh, and river, where, again and again, in the bitterness of baffled striving, the untiring pilgrim pushed onward toward the goal which he was never to attain. America owes him an enduring memory; for, in this masculine figure, she sees the pioneer who guided her to the possession of her richest heritage.

III

THE COMING OF FRONTENAC TO CANADA [4]
(1672)

COUNT FRONTENAC came of an ancient and noble race, said to have been of Basque origin. His father held a high post in the household of Louis XIII, who became the child's godfather, and gave him his own name. At the age of fifteen, the young Louis showed an uncontrollable passion for the life of a soldier. He was sent to the seat of war in Holland, to serve under the Prince of Orange. At the age of nineteen, he was a volunteer at the siege of Hesdin; in the next year he was at Arras, where he distinguished himself during a sortie of the garrison; in the next, he took part in the siege of Aire; and, in the next, in those of Callioure and Perpignan. At the age of twenty-three, he was made colonel of the regiment of Normandy, which he commanded in repeated battles and sieges of the Italian campaign. He was several times

[4] From Chapters I and II of "Count Frontenac and New France Under Louis XIV." Copyright, 1877, by Francis Parkman. Published by Little, Brown & Company.

wounded, and in 1646 he had an arm broken at the siege of Orbitello. In the same year, when twenty-six years old, he was raised to the rank of maréchal de camp, equivalent to that of brigadier-general. A year or two later we find him at Paris, at the house of his father, on the Quai des Célestins.

In the same neighborhood lived La Grange-Trianon, Sieur de Neuville, a widower of fifty, with one child, a daughter of sixteen, whom he had placed in the charge of his relative, Madame de Bouthillier. Frontenac fell in love with her. Madam de Bouthillier opposed the match, and told La Grange that he might do better for his daughter than marry her to a man who, say what he might, had but twenty thousand francs a year. La Grange was weak and vacillating: sometimes he listened to his prudent kinswoman, and sometimes to the eager suitor; treated him as a son-in-law, carried love messages from him to his daughter, and ended by refusing him her hand, and ordering her to renounce him on pain of being immured in a convent. Neither Frontenac nor his mistress was of a pliant temper. In the neighborhood was the little church of St. Pierre aux Boeufs, which had the privilege of uniting couples without the consent of their parents; and here, on a Wednesday in October, 1648, the lovers were married in presence of a number of Frontenac's relatives. La Grange was furious at the discovery; but his anger soon cooled, and complete reconciliation followed.

The happiness of the newly wedded pair was short. Love soon changed to aversion, at least on the part of the bride. She was not of a tender nature; her temper was imperious, and she had a restless craving for excitement. Frontenac, on his part, was the most wayward and headstrong of men. She bore him a son; but maternal cares were not to her liking. . . .

At Versailles there is a portrait of a lady, beautiful and young. She is painted as Minerva, a plumed helmet on her head, and a shield on her arm. In a corner of the canvas is written Anne de La Grange-Trianon, Comtesse de Frontenac. This blooming goddess was the wife of the future governor of Canada.

Madame de Frontenac, at the age of about twenty, was a favorite companion of Mademoiselle de Montpensier, the grand-daughter of Henry IV and a daughter of the weak and dastardly Gaston, Duke of Orleans. Nothing in French annals has found more readers than the story of the exploit of this spirited princess at Orleans during the civil war of the Fronde. Her cousin Condé, chief of the revolt, had found favor in her eyes; and she had espoused his cause against her cousin, the King. . . .

In 1669, a Venetian embassy came to France to beg for aid against the Turks, who for more than two years had attacked Candia in overwhelming force. The ambassadors offered to place their own troops under French command, and they asked Turenne to name a general officer equal to the task. Frontenac had the signal honor of being chosen by the first soldier of Europe for this most arduous and difficult position. He went accordingly. The result increased his reputation for ability and courage; but Candia was doomed, and its chief fortress fell into the hands of the infidels, after a protracted struggle, which is said to have cost them a hundred and eighty thousand men.

Three years later Frontenac received the appointment of Governor and Lieutenant-General for the King in all New France. "He was," says Saint-Simon, "a man of excellent parts, living much in society, and completely ruined. He found it hard to bear the imperious temper of his wife and he was given the government of Canada to deliver him from her, and afford him some means of living." Certain scandalous songs of the day assign a different motive for his appointment. Louis XIV was enamored of Madame de Montespan. She had once smiled upon Frontenac; and it is said that the jealous King gladly embraced the opportunity of removing from his presence and from hers a lover who had forestalled him.

Frontenac's wife had no thought of following him across the sea, a more congenial life awaiting her at home. . . .

Frontenac was fifty-two years old when he landed at Quebec. If time had done little to cure his many faults, it had done nothing to weaken the springs of his unconquerable vitality. In his ripe middle age he was as keen, fiery, and perversely headstrong as when he quarreled with Prefontaine in the hall at St. Fargeau.

Had nature disposed him to melancholy, there was much in his position to awaken it. A man of courts and camps, born and bred in the focus of a most gorgeous civilization, he was banished to the ends of the earth, among savage hordes and half-reclaimed forests, to exchange the splen-

dors of St. Germain and the dawning glories
of Versailles for a stern gray rock, haunted
by somber priests, rugged merchants and traders,
blanketed Indians, and wild bushrangers. But
Frontenac was a man of action. He wasted no
time in vain regrets, and set himself to his work
with the elastic vigor of youth. His first impressions had been very favorable. When, as he
sailed up the St. Lawrence, the basin of Quebec
opened before him, his imagination kindled with
the grandeur of the scene. "I never," he wrote,
"saw anything more superb than the position of
this town. It could not be better situated as
the future capital of a great empire."

IV

THE DEATH OF ISAAC JOGUES [5]
(1646)

LATE in the autumn a party of the Indians
set forth on their yearly deer-hunt, and Jogues
was ordered to go with them. Shivering and
half-famished, he followed them through the chill
November forest, and shared their wild bivouac
in the depths of the wintry desolation. The game

[5] From Chapters XVI and XX of "The Jesuits in North
America." Copyright, 1867, 1895, by Francis Parkman.
Published by Little, Brown & Company. The site of Jogues's
martyrdom is near Auriesville in the Mohawk valley, where
a memorial chapel in his honor is now maintained, the Rev.
John J. Wynne, S. J., having been active in securing and
maintaining it.

they took was devoted to Areskoui, their god, and eaten in his honor. Jogues would not taste the meat offered to a demon; and thus he starved in the midst of plenty. At night, when the kettle was slung, and the savage crew made merry around their fire, he crouched in a corner of the hunt, gnawed by hunger, and pierced to the bone with cold. They thought his presence unpropitious to their hunting, and the women especially hated him. His demeanor at once astonished and incensed his masters. He brought them fire-wood, like a squaw; he did their bidding without a murmur, and patiently bore their abuse; but when they mocked at his God, and laughed at his devotions, their slave assumed an air and tone of authority, and sternly rebuked them.

He would sometimes escape from "this Babylon," as he calls the hut, and wander in the forest, telling his beads and repeating passages of Scripture. In a remote and lonely spot he cut the bark in the form of the cross from the trunk of a great tree; and here he made his prayers. This living martyr, half-clad in shaggy furs, kneeling on the snow among the icicled rocks and beneath the gloomy pines, bowing in adoration before the emblem of the faith in which was his only consolation and his only hope, is alike a theme for the pen and a subject for the pencil. . . .

He remained two days, half-stifled, in this foul lurking-place,[6] while the Indians, furious at his escape, ransacked the settlement in vain to find him. They came off to the vessel, and so terrified the officers that Jogues was sent on

[6] Near Albany, or Fort Orange, as it was then called.

shore at night, and led to the fort. Here he was hidden in the garret of a house occupied by a miserly old man, to whose charge he was consigned. Food was sent to him; but, as his host appropriated the larger part to himself, Jogues was nearly starved. There was a compartment of his garret, separated from the rest by a partition of boards. Here the old Dutchman, who, like many others of the settlers, carried on a trade with the Mohawks, kept a quantity of goods for that purpose; and hither he often brought his customers. The boards of the partition had shrunk, leaving wide crevices; and Jogues could plainly see the Indians, as they passed between him and the light. They, on their part, might as easily have seen him, if he had not, when he heard them entering the house, hidden himself behind some barrels in the corner, where he would sometimes remain crouched for hours, in a constrained and painful posture, half-suffocated with heat, and afraid to move a limb. His wounded leg began to show dangerous symptoms; but he was relieved by the care of a Dutch surgeon of the fort. The minister, Megapolensis, also visited him, and did all in his power for the comfort of his Catholic brother, with whom he seems to have been well pleased, and whom he calls "a very learned scholar."

When Jogues had remained for six weeks in this hiding-place, his Dutch friends succeeded in satisfying his Indian masters by the payment of a large ransom. A vessel from Manhattan, now New York, soon after brought up an order from the Director-General, Kieft, that he should be sent to him. Accordingly, he was placed in a small vessel, which carried him down the Hudson. The Dutch on board treated him with great kindness; and, to do him honor, named after him one of the islands in the river. At Manhattan he found a dilapidated fort, garrisoned by sixty soldiers, and containing a stone church and the Director-General's house, together with storehouses and barracks. Near it were ranges of small houses, occupied chiefly by mechanics and laborers; while the dwellings of the remaining colonists, numbering in all four or five hundred, were scattered here and there on the island and the neighboring shores. The settlers were of different sects and nations, but chiefly Dutch Calvinists. Kieft told his guest that eighteen different languages were spoken at Manhattan. The colonists were in the midst of a bloody Indian war, brought on by their own besotted cruelty; and while Jogues was at the fort, some forty of the Dutchmen were killed on the neighboring farms, and many barns and houses burned.

The Director-General, with a humanity that was far from usual with him, exchanged Jogues's squalid and savage dress for a suit of Dutch cloth, and gave him passage in a small vessel which was then about to sail. . . .

Jogues became a center of curiosity and reverence. He was summoned to Paris. The Queen, Anne of Austria, wished to see him; and when the persecuted slave of the Mohawks was conducted into her presence, she kissed his mutilated hands, while the ladies of the court thronged around to do him homage. We are told, and no doubt with truth, that these honors were unwelcome to the modest and single-hearted missionary, who thought only of returning to his work of converting the Indians. A priest with any deformity of body is debarred from saying mass. The teeth and knives of the Iroquois had inflicted an injury worse than the tortures imagined, for they had robbed Jogues of the privilege which was the chief consolation of his life; but the Pope, by a special dispensation, restored it to him, and with the opening spring he sailed again for Canada. . . .

In the evening—it was the eighteenth of October—Jogues, smarting with his wounds and bruises, was sitting in one of the lodges, when an Indian entered, and asked him to a feast. To refuse would have been an offense. He arose and followed the savage, who led him to the lodge of the Bear chief. Jogues bent his head to enter, when another Indian, standing concealed within, at the side of the doorway, struck at him with a hatchet. An Iroquois, called by the French Le Berger, who seems to have followed in order to defend him, bravely held out his arm to ward off the blow; but the hatchet cut through it, and sank into the missionary's brain. He fell at the feet of his murderer, who at once finished the work by hacking off his head. Lalande was left in suspense all night, and in the morning was killed in a similar manner. The bodies of the two Frenchmen were then thrown into the Mohawk, and their heads displayed on the points of the palisade which enclosed the town.

Thus died Isaac Jogues, one of the purest examples of Roman Catholic virtue which this western continent has seen.

V

WHY NEW FRANCE FAILED [7]

New France was all head. Under king, noble, and Jesuit, the lank, lean body would not thrive. Even commerce wore the sword, decked itself with badges of nobility, aspired to forest seigniories and hordes of savage retainers. Along the borders of the sea an adverse power was strengthening and widening, with slow but stedfast growth, full of blood and muscle—a body without a head. Each had its strength, each its weakness, each its own modes of vigorous life: but the one was fruitful, the other barren; the one instinct with hope, the other darkening with shadows of despair.

By name, local position, and character one of these communities of freemen stands forth as the most conspicuous representative of this antagonism—liberty and absolutism, New England and New France. The one was the offspring of a triumphant government; the other, of an opprest and fugitive people: the one, an unflinching champion of the Roman Catholic reaction; the other, a vanguard of the Reform. Each followed its natural laws of growth, and each came to its natural results. Vitalized by the principles of its foundation, the Puritan commonwealth

<hr>

[7] From the introduction to "The Pioneers of France in the New World." Copyright, 1865, 1885, by Francis Parkman. Published by Little, Brown & Company.

grew apace. New England was preeminently the land of material progress. Here the prize was within every man's reach; patient industry need never doubt its reward; nay, in defiance of the four gospels, assiduity in pursuit of gain was promoted to the rank of a duty, and thrift and godliness were linked in equivocal wedlock. Politically she was free; socially she suffered from that subtile and searching oppression which the dominant opinion of a free community may exercise over the members who compose it. As a whole, she grew upon the gaze of the world, a signal example of expansive energy; but she has not been fruitful in those salient and striking forms of character which often give a dramatic life to the annals of nations far less prosperous.

We turn to New France, and all is reversed. Here was a bold attempt to crush under the exactions of a grasping hierarchy, to stifle under the curbs and trappings of a feudal monarchy a people compassed by influences of the wildest freedom—whose schools were the forest and the sea, whose trade was an armed barter with savages, and whose daily life a lesson of lawless independence. But this fierce spirit had its vent. The story of New France is from the first a story of war: of war—for so her founders believed—with the adversary of mankind himself; war with savage tribes and potent forest commonwealths; war with the encroaching powers of heresy and of England. Her brave, unthinking people were stamped with the soldier's virtues and the soldier's faults; and in their leaders were displayed, on a grand and novel stage, the energies, aspirations, and passions which belong to hopes vast and vague, ill-restricted powers, and stations of command.

The growth of New England was a result of the aggregate efforts of a busy multitude, each in his narrow circle toiling for himself, to gather competence or wealth. The expansion of New France was the achievement of a gigantic ambition striving to grasp a continent. It was a vain attempt. Long and valiantly her chiefs upheld their cause, leading to battle a vassal population, warlike as themselves. Borne down by numbers from without, wasted by corruption from within, New France fell at last; and out of her fall grew revolutions whose influence to this hour is felt through every nation of the civilized world.

The French dominion is a memory of the past; and when we evoke its departed shades, they rise upon us from their graves in strange, romantic guise. Again their ghostly camp-fires seem to burn, and the fitful light is cast around on lord and vassal and black-robed priest, mingled with wild forms of savage warriors, knit in close fellowship on the same stern errand. A boundless vision grows upon us; an untamed continent; vast wastes of forest verdure; mountains silent in primeval sleep; river, lake, and glimmering pool; wilderness oceans mingling with the sky. Such was the domain which France conquered for civilization. Plumed helmets gleamed in the shade of its forests, priestly vestments in its dens and fastnesses of ancient barbarism. Men steeped in antique learning, pale with the close breath of the cloister, here spent the noon and evening of their lives, ruled savage hordes with a mild, parental sway, and stood serene before the direst shapes of death. Men of courtly nurture, heirs to the polish of a far-reaching ancestry, here, with their dauntless hardihood, put to shame the boldest sons of toil.

VI

THE RETURN OF THE COUREURS-DE-BOIS [8]

IT was a curious scene when a party of *coureurs de bois* returned from their rovings. Montreal was their harboring place, and they conducted themselves much like the crew of a man-of-war paid off after a long voyage. As long as their beaver-skins lasted, they set no bounds to their riot. Every house in the place, we are told, was turned into a drinking-shop. The newcomers were bedizened with a strange mixture of French and Indian finery; while some of them, with instincts more thoroughly savage, stalked about the streets as naked as a Pottawottamie or a Sioux. The clamor of tongues was prodigious, and gambling and drinking filled the day and the night. When at last they were sober again, they sought absolution for their sins; nor could the priests venture to bear too hard on their unruly penitents, lest they should break wholly

with the church and dispense thenceforth with
her sacraments.

Under such leaders as Du Lhut, the *coureurs
de bois* built forts of palisades at various points
throughout the West and Northwest. They had
a post of this sort at Detroit some time before
its permanent settlement, as well as others on
Lake Superior and in the valley of the Mississippi. They occupied them as long as it suited
their purposes, and then abandoned them to the
next comer. Michillimackinac was, however,
their chief resort; and thence they would set
out, two or three together, to roam for hundreds
of miles through the endless meshwork of inter-
locking lakes and rivers which seams the northern
wilderness.

No wonder that a year or two of bushranging
spoiled them for civilization. Tho not a very
valuable member of society, and tho a thorn in
the side of princes and rulers, the *coureur de bois*
had his uses, at least from an artistic point of
view; and his strange figure, sometimes brutally
savage, but oftener marked with the lines of a
daredevil courage, and a reckless, thoughtless
gaiety, will always be joined to the memories of
that grand world of woods which the nineteenth
century is fast civilizing out of existence. At
least, he is picturesque, and with his redskin
companion serves to animate forest scenery.
Perhaps he could sometimes feel, without knowing that he felt them, the charms of the savage
nature that had adopted him.

Rude as he was, her voice may not always
have been meaningless for one who knew her
haunts so well; deep recesses where, veiled in

foliage, some wild shy rivulet steals with timid
music through breathless caves of verdure; gulfs
where feathered crags rise like castle walls,
where the noonday sun pierces with keen rays
athwart the torrent, and the mossed arms of
fallen pines cast wavering shadows on the il-
lumined foam; pools of liquid crystal turned
emerald in the reflected green of impending
woods; rocks on whose rugged front the gleam
of sunlit waters dances in quivering light; ancient trees hurled headlong by the storm to dam
the raging stream with their forlorn and savage
ruin; or the stern depths of immemorial forests,
dim and silent as a cavern, columned with innumerable trunks, each like an Atlas upholding its
world of leaves, and sweating perpetual moisture
down its dark and channelled rind; some strong
in youth, some grisly with decrepit age, night-
mares of strange distortion, gnarled and knotted
with wens and goitres; roots intertwined beneath
like serpents petrified in an agony of contorted
strife; green and glistening mosses carpeting the
rough ground, mantling the rocks, turning pulpy
stumps to mounds of verdure, and swathing fallen
trunks as, bent in the impotence of rottenness,
they lie outstretched over knoll and hollow, like
moldering reptiles of the primeval world, while
around, and on and through them, springs the
young growth that fattens on their decay—the
forest devouring its own dead. Or, to turn from
its funereal shade to the light and life of the
open woodland, the sheen of sparkling lakes, and
mountains basking in the glory of the summer
noon, flecked by the shadows of passing clouds
that sail on snowy wings across the azure.

Yet it would be false coloring to paint the half-savage *coureur de bois* as a romantic lover of nature. He liked the woods because they emancipated him from restraint. He liked the lounging ease of the camp-fire, and the license of Indian villages. His life has a dark and ugly side.

GEORGE WILLIAM CURTIS

Born in 1824, died in 1892; joined the Brook Farm Community; traveled in Europe in 1846-50; became connected with the New York *Tribune* in 1850; editor of *Putnam's Monthly* in 1852-57, with *Harper's Magazine* in 1854, and with *Harper's Weekly* in 1863; prominent advocate of civil service reform, being one of the commissioners appointed by President Grant in 1871, but resigned on account of differences with the President; president of the State Civil Service League in 1880, and of the National Civil Service Reform League afterward until his death; published "Nile Notes of a Howadji" in 1851, "Lotus Eating" in 1852, "Potiphar Papers" in 1853, "Prue and I" in 1856.

OUR COUSIN THE CURATE [1]

OUR cousin the curate loved, while he was yet a boy, Flora, of the sparkling eyes and the ringing voice. His devotion was absolute. Flora was flattered, because all the girls, as I said, worshiped him; but she was a gay, glancing girl, who had invaded the student's heart with her audacious brilliancy, and was half-surprised that she had subdued it. Our cousin—for I never think of him as my cousin only—wasted away under the fervor of his passion. His life exhaled an incense before her. He wrote poems to her, and sang them under her window, in the summer moonlight. He brought her flowers and precious gifts. When he had nothing else to give, he gave her his love in a homage so eloquent and

[1] From Chapter VII of "Prue and I."

beautiful that the worship was like the worship of the wise men. The gay Flora was proud and superb. She was a girl, and the bravest and best boy loved her. She was young, and the wisest and truest youth loved her. They lived together, we all lived together, in the happy valley of childhood. We looked forward to manhood as island-poets look across the sea, believing that the whole world beyond is a blest Araby of spices.

The months went by, and the young love continued. Our cousin and Flora were only children still, and there was no engagement. The elders looked upon the intimacy as natural and mutually beneficial. It would help soften the boy and strengthen the girl; and they took for granted that softness and strength were precisely what were wanted. It is a great pity that men and women forget that they have been children. Parents are apt to be foreigners to their sons and daughters. Maturity is the gate of paradise, which shuts behind us; and our memories are gradually weaned from the glories in which our nativity was cradled.

The months went by, the children grew older, and they constantly loved. Now Prue always smiles at one of my theories; she is entirely skeptical of it; but it is, nevertheless, my opinion that men love most passionately, and women most permanently. Men love at first and most warmly; women love last and longest. This is natural enough; for nature makes women to be won, and men to win. Men are the active, positive force, and therefore, they are more ardent and demonstrative. . . .

Why our cousin should have loved the gay Flora so ardently was hard to say; but that he did so, was not difficult to see. He went away to college. He wrote the most eloquent and passionate letters; and when he returned in vacations, he had no eyes, ears, nor heart for any other being. I rarely saw him, for I was living away from our early home, and was busy in a store — learning to be bookkeeper — but I heard afterward from himself the whole story.

One day when he came home for the holidays, he found a young foreigner with Flora—a handsome youth, brilliant and graceful. I have asked Prue a thousand times why women adore soldiers and foreigners. She says it is because they love heroism and are romantic. A soldier is professionally a hero, says Prue, and a foreigner is associated with all unknown and beautiful regions. I hope there is no worse reason. . . .

Our cousin came home and found Flora and the young foreigner conversing. The young foreigner had large, soft, black eyes, and the dusky skin of the tropics. His manner was languid and fascinating, courteous and reserved. It assumed a natural supremacy, and you felt as if here were a young prince traveling before he came into possession of his realm. . . .

Our cousin the curate no sooner saw the tropical stranger and marked his impression upon Flora than he felt the end. As the shaft struck his heart, his smile was sweeter, and his homage even more poetic and reverential. I doubt if Flora understood him or herself. She did not know, what he instinctively perceived, that she loved him less. But there are no degrees in love;

when it is less than absolute and supreme, it is nothing. Our cousin and Flora were not formally engaged, but their betrothal was understood by all of us as a thing of course. He did not allude to the stranger; but as day followed day, he saw with every nerve all that passed. Gradually—so gradually that she scarcely noticed it—our cousin left Flora more and more with the soft-eyed stranger, whom he saw she preferred. His treatment of her was so full of tact, he still walked and talked with her so familiarly that she was not troubled by any fear that he saw what she hardly saw herself. Therefore, she was not obliged to conceal anything from him or from herself; but all the soft currents of her heart were setting toward the West Indian. Our cousin's cheek grew paler, and his soul burned and wasted within him. His whole future—all his dream of life—had been founded upon his love. It was a stately palace built upon the sand, and now the sand was sliding away. I have read somewhere that love will sacrifice everything but itself. But our cousin sacrificed his love to the happiness of his mistress. He ceased to treat her as peculiarly his own. He made no claim in word or manner that everybody might not have made. He did not refrain from seeing her, or speaking of her as of all his other friends; and, at length, altho no one could say how or when the change had been made, it was evident and understood that he was no more her lover, but that both were the best of friends.

He still wrote to her occasionally from college, and his letters were those of a friend, not of a lover. He could not reproach her. I do not believe any man is secretly surprised that a woman ceases to love him. Her love is a heavenly favor won by no desert of his. If it passes, he can no more complain than a flower when the sunshine leaves it.

Before our cousin left college Flora was married to the tropical stranger. It was the brightest of June days, and the summer smiled upon the bride. There were roses in her hand and orange flowers in her hair, and the village church bell rang out over the peaceful fields. The warm sunshine lay upon the landscape like God's blessing, and Prue and I, not yet married ourselves, stood at an open window in the old meeting-house, hand in hand, while the young couple spoke their vows. Prue says that brides are always beautiful, and I, who remember Prue herself upon her wedding-day—how can I deny it? Truly, the gay Flora was lovely that summer morning, and the throng was happy in the old church. But it was very sad to me, altho I only suspected then what now I know. I shed no tears at my own wedding, but I did at Flora's, altho I knew she was marrying a soft-eyed youth whom she dearly loved, and who, I doubt not, dearly loved her.

Among the group of her nearest friends was our cousin the curate. When the ceremony was ended, he came to shake her hand with the rest. His face was calm, and his smile sweet, and his manner unconstrained. Flora did not blush— why should she?—but shook his hand warmly, and thanked him for his good wishes. Then they all sauntered down the aisle together; there were some tears with the smiles among the other friends; our cousin handed the bride into her carriage, shook hands with the husband, closed the door, and Flora drove away.

I have never seen her since; I do not even know if she be living still. But I shall always remember her as she looked that June morning, holding roses in her hand, and wreathed with orange flowers. Dear Flora! it was no fault of hers that she loved one man more than another: she could not be blamed for not preferring our cousin to the West Indian: there is no fault in the story, it is only a tragedy.

Our cousin carried all the collegiate honors— but without exciting jealousy or envy. He was so really the best, that his companions were anxious he should have the sign of his superiority. He studied hard, he thought much, and wrote well. There was no evidence of any blight upon his ambition or career, but after living quietly in the country for some time, he went to Europe and traveled. When he returned, he resolved to study law, but presently relinquished it. Then he collected materials for a history, but suffered them to lie unused. Somehow the mainspring was gone. He used to come and pass weeks with Prue and me. His coming made the children happy, for he sat with them, and talked and played with them all day long, as one of themselves. . . .

At length our cousin went abroad again to Europe. It was many years ago that we watched him sail away, and when Titbottom, and Prue, and I went home to dinner, the grace that was said that day was a fervent prayer for our cousin the curate. Many an evening afterward, the children wanted him, and cried themselves to sleep calling upon his name. Many an evening still our talk flags into silence as we sit before the fire, and Prue puts down her knitting and takes my hand, as if she knew my thoughts, altho we do not name his name.

He wrote us letters as he wandered about the world. They were affectionate letters, full of observation, and thought, and description. He lingered longest in Italy, but he said his conscience accused him of yielding to the sirens; and he declared that his life was running uselessly away. At last he came to England. He was charmed with everything, and the climate was even kinder to him than that of Italy. He went to all the famous places, and saw many of the famous Englishmen, and wrote that he felt England to be his home. Burying himself in the ancient gloom of a university town, altho past the prime of life, he studied like an ambitious boy. He said again that his life had been wine poured upon the ground, and he felt guilty. And so our cousin became a curate. . . .

Our children have forgotten their old playmate; but I am sure if there be any children in his parish, over the sea, they love our cousin the curate, and watch eagerly for his coming. Does his step falter now, I wonder; is that long fair hair gray; is that laugh as musical in those distant homes as it used to be in our nursery; has England among all her great and good men any man so noble as our cousin the curate?

The great book is unwritten; the great deeds are undone; in no biographical dictionary will you find the name of our cousin the curate. Is his life therefore lost? Have his powers been wasted?

I do not dare to say it, for I see Bourne on the pinnacle of prosperity, but still looking sadly for his castles in Spain; I see Titbottom, an old deputy bookkeeper, whom nobody knows, but with his chivalric heart loyal to children, his generous and humane spirit, full of sweet hope and faith and devotion; I see the superb Auriel, so lovely that the Indians would call her a smile of the Great Spirit, and as beneficent as a saint of the calendar—how shall I say what is lost and what is won. I know that in every way and by all His preachers God is served and His purposes accomplished. How shall I explain or understand? I, who am only an old bookkeeper in an old cravat.

ARTEMUS WARD

Born in 1834, died in England in 1867; his real name Charles Farrar Browne; noted as a humorous lecturer here and in England; published "Artemus Ward: His Book" in 1862; "Artemus Ward: His Travels" in 1865; "Artemus Ward in London" in 1867.

FORREST AS OTHELLO[1]

DURIN a recent visit to New York the under-sined went to see Edwin Forrest. As I am into the moral show biziness myself I ginrally go to Barnum's moral museum, where only moral pee-ple air admitted, partickly on Wednesday arter-noons. But this time I thot I'd go and see Ed. Ed has bin actin out on the stage for many years. There is varis 'pinions about his actin, English-men ginrally bleevin that he's far superior to Mister Macready; but on one pint all agree, & that is that Ed draws like a six-ox team. Ed was actin at Niblo's Garding, which looks con-siderable more like a parster than a garding, but let that pars. I sot down in the pit, took out my spectacles and commenced peroosin the eve-nin's bill. The awjince was all-fired large & the boxes was full of the elitty of New York. Sev-eral opery glasses was leveled at me by Gotham's fairest darters, but I didn't let on as tho I noticed it, tho mebby I did take out my sixteen-dollar silver watch & brandish it round more than was necessary. But the best of us has our weaknesses & if a man has gewelry let him show it. As I was peroosin the bill a grave young

[1] From "Artemus Ward: His Book."

man who sot near me axed me if I'd ever seen
Forrest dance the Essence of Old Virginny.
"He's immense in that," sed the young man.
"He also does a fair champion jig," the young
man continnered, "but his Big Thing is the
Essence of Old Virginny." Sez I, "Fair youth,
do you know what I'd do with you if you was
my sun?"

"No," sez he.

"Wall," sez I, "I'd appint your funeral to-
morrow arternoon, & the *korps should be ready.*
You're too smart to live on this yerth."

He didn't try any more of his capers on me.
But another pussylanermuss individooul in a red
vest and patent leather boots told me his name
was Bill Astor & axed me to lend him 50 cents
till early in the mornin. I told him I'd probly
send it round to him before he retired to his
virtoous couch, but if I didn't he might look for
it next fall as soon as I'd cut my corn.

The orchestry was now fiddling with all their
might & as the peeple didn't understan anything
about it they applaudid versifrusly. Presently
old Ed cum out. The play was Otheller or More
of Veniss. Otheller was writ by Wm. Shakspeer.
The seene is laid in Veniss. Otheller was a likely
man & was a ginral in the Veniss army. He
eloped with Desdemony, a darter of the Hon.
Mr. Brabantio who represented one of the back
districks in the Veneshun legislater. Old Brabantio was as mad as thunder at this & tore
round considerable, but finally cooled down, telling Otheller, howsoever, that Desdemony had
come it over her par, & that he had better look
out or she'd come it over him likewise.

Mr. and Mrs. Otheller git along very comfort-able-like for a spell. She is sweet-tempered and lovin—a nice, sensible female, never goin in for he-female conventions, green cotton umbrellers, and pickled beats. Otheller is a good provider and thinks all the world of his wife. She has a lazy time of it, the hird girl doin all the cookin and washin. Desdemony in fact don't have to git the water to wash her own hands with. But a low cuss named Iago, who I bleeve wants to git Otheller out of his snug government birth, now goes to work & upsets the Otheller family in most outrajus stile. Iago falls in with a brainless youth named Roderigo & wins all his money at poker. (Iago allers played foul.) He thus got money enuff to carry out his onprincipled skeem. Mike Cassio, a Irishman, is selecte' as a tool by Iago. Mike was a clever feller & a orficer in Otheller's army. He liked his tods too well, howsoever, & they floored him as they have many other promisin young men. Iago injuces Mike to drink with him, Iago slily throwin his whiskey over his shoulder. Mike gits as drunk as a biled owl & allows that he can lick a yard full of the Veneshun fancy before break-fast, without sweating a hair. He meets Rode-rigo & proceeds for to smash him. A feller named Mentano undertakes to slap Cassio, when that infatooated person runs his sword into him. That miserble man, Iago, pretends to be very sorry to see Mike conduck hisself in this way & undertakes to smooth the thing over to Othel-ler, who rushes in with a drawn sword & wants to know what's up. Iago cunningly tells his story & Otheller tells Mike that he thinks a good deal of him but that he cant train no more in his regiment. Desdemony sympathizes with poor Mike & interceds for him with Otheller. Iago makes him bleeve she does this because she thinks more of Mike than she does of hisself. Otheller swallers Iagos lying tail & goes to makin a noosence of hisself ginrally. He worries poor Desdemony terrible by his vile insinuations & finally smothers her to death with a piller. Mrs. Iago comes in just as Otheller has finished the fowl deed & givs him fits right & left, showin him that he has been orfully gulled by her miserble cuss of a husband. Iago cums in & his wife commences rakin him down also, when he stabs her. Otheller jaws him a spell & then cuts a small hole in his stummick with his sword. Iago pints to Desdemony's deth bed & goes orf with a sardonic smile onto his countenance. Otheller tells the peeple that he has dun the state some service & they know it; axes them to do as fair a thing as they can for him under the circumstances, & kills hisself with a fish-knife, which is the most sensible thing he can do. This is a breef skedule of the synopsis of the play.

Edwin Forrest is a grate acter. I thot I saw Otheller before me all the time he was actin &, when the curtin fell, I found my spectacles was still mistened with salt-water, which had run from my eyes while poor Desdemony was dyin. Betsy Jane—Betsy Jane! let us pray that our domestic bliss may never be busted up by a Iago!

Edwin Forrest makes money acting out on the stage. He gits five hundred dollars a nite & his board & washin. I wish I had such a Forrest in my Garding!

THOMAS BAILEY ALDRICH

Born in 1836; died in 1908; a literary man in New York in early life; removing to Boston, became editor of *Every Saturday* in 1870-74; editor of the *Atlantic Monthly* in 1881-1890; among his works "The Ballad of Babie Bell" published in 1856, "Cloth of Gold" in 1874, "Flower and Thorn" in 1876, "Story of a Bad Boy" in 1870, "Marjorie Daw" in 1873, "Prudence Palfrey" in 1874, "The Queen of Sheba" in 1877, "The Stillwater Tragedy" in 1880, "From Ponkapog to Pesth" in 1883, "The Sister's Tragedy in 1891.

I

A SUNRISE IN STILLWATER [1]

IT is close upon daybreak. The great wall of pines and hemlocks that keep off the east wind from Stillwater stretches black and indeterminate against the sky. At intervals a dull, metallic sound, like the guttural twang of a violin string, rises from the frog-invested swamp skirting the highway. Suddenly the birds stir in their nests over there in the woodland, and break into that wild jargoning chorus with which they herald the advent of a new day. In the apple orchards and among the plum-trees of the few gardens in Stillwater the wrens and the robins and the blue-jays catch up the crystal crescendo, and what a melodious racket they make of it with their fifes and flutes and flageolets!

[1] From Chapter I of "The Stillwater Tragedy." Copyright, 1880, by Thomas Bailey Aldrich. Published by Houghton, Mifflin Company.

The village lies in a trance like death. Possibly not a soul hears this music, unless it is the watchers at the bedside of Mr. Leonard Tappleton, the richest man in town, who has lain dying these three days, and can not last till sunrise. Or perhaps some mother, drowsily hushing her wakeful baby, pauses a moment and listens vacantly to the birds singing. But who else?

The hubbub suddenly ceases—ceases as suddenly as it began—and all is still again in the woodland. But it is not so dark as before. A faint glow of white light is discernible behind the ragged line of the tree tops. The deluge of darkness is receding from the face of the earth, as the mighty waters receded of old.

The roofs and tall factory chimneys of Stillwater are slowly taking shape in the gloom. Is that a cemetery coming into view yonder, with its ghostly architecture of obelisks and broken columns and huddled headstones? No, that is only Slocum's marble yard, with the finished and unfinished work heaped up like snowdrifts—a cemetery in embryo. Here and there in an outlying farm a lantern glimmers in the barn-yard: the cattle are having their fodder betimes. Scarlet-capped chanticleer gets himself on the nearest rail fence and lifts up his rancorous voice like some irate old cardinal launching the curse of Rome. Something crawls swiftly along the gray of the serpentine turnpike — a cart, with the driver lashing a jaded horse. A quick wind goes shivering by, and is lost in the forest.

Now a narrow strip of two-colored gold stretches along the horizon.

Stillwater is gradually coming to its senses.

The sun has begun to twinkle on the gilt cross of the Catholic chapel and make itself known to the doves in the stone belfry on the South Church. The patches of cobweb that here and there cling tremulously to the coarse grass of the inundated meadows have turned into silver nets, and the mill-pond—it will be steel-blue later—is as smooth and white as if it had been paved with one vast unbroken slab out of Slocum's marble yard. Through a row of buttonwoods on the northern skirt of the village is seen a square, lap-streaked building, painted a disagreeable brown, and surrounded on three sides by a platform — one of seven or eight similar stations strung like Indian beads on a branch thread of the Great Sagamore Railway.

Listen! That is the jingle of the bells on the baker's cart as it begins its rounds. From innumerable chimneys the curled smoke gives evidence that the thrifty housewife—or, what is rarer in Stillwater, the hired girl—has lighted the kitchen fire.

The chimney-stack of one house at the end of a small court—the last house on the easterly edge of the village, and standing quite alone— sends up no smoke. Yet the carefully trained ivy over the porch, and the lemon verbena in a tub at the foot of the steps, intimate that the place is not unoccupied. Moreover, the little schooner which acts as weathercock on one of the gables, and is now heading due west, has a new topsail. It is a story-and-a-half cottage, with a large expanse of roof, which, covered with porous, unpainted shingles, seems to repel the sunshine that now strikes full upon it. The upper and lower blinds on the main building, as well as those on the extensions, are tightly closed. The sun appears to beat in vain at the casements of this silent house, which has a curiously sullen and defiant air, as if it had desperately and successfully barricaded itself against the approach of morning; yet if one were standing in the room that leads from the bedchamber on the ground floor—the room with the latticed window—one would see a ray of light thrust through a chink of the shutters, and pointing like a human finger at an object which lies by the hearth.

This finger, gleaming, motionless, and awful in its precision, points to the body of old Mr. Lemuel Shackford, who lies there dead in his night-dress, with a gash across his forehead.

In the darkness of that summer night a deed darker than the night itself had been done in Stillwater.

II

THE FIGHT AT SLATTER'S HILL [2]

THE memory of man, even that of the oldest inhabitant runneth not back to the time when there did not exist a feud between the North End and the South End boys of Rivermouth.

The origin of the feud is involved in mystery;

[2] From Chapter XIII of "The Story of a Bad Boy." Copyright, 1869, 1877, by Thomas Bailey Aldrich. Published by Houghton, Mifflin Company.

it is impossible to say which party was the first aggressor in the far-off anterevolutionary ages; but the fact remains that the youngsters of those antipodal sections entertained a mortal hatred for each other, and that this hatred had been handed down from generation to generation, like Miles Standish's punch-bowl.

I know not what laws, natural or unnatural, regulated the warmth of the quarrel; but at some seasons it raged more violently than at others. This winter both parties were unusually lively and antagonistic. Great was the wrath of the South-Enders when they discovered that the North-Enders had thrown up a fort on the crown of Slatter's Hill.

Slatter's Hill, or No-man's-land, as it was generally called, was a rise of ground covering, perhaps, an acre and a quarter, situated on an imaginary line marking the boundary between the two districts. An immense stratum of granite, which here and there thrust out a wrinkled boulder, prevented the site from being used for building purposes. The street ran on either side of the hill, from one part of which a quantity of rock had been removed to form the underpinning of the new jail. This excavation made the approach from that point all but impossible, especially when the ragged ledges were a-glitter with ice. You see what a spot it was for a snow-fort.

One evening twenty or thirty of the North-Enders quietly took possession of Slatter's Hill, and threw up a strong line of breastworks. The rear of the entrenchment, being protected by the quarry, was left open. The walls were four feet

high, and twenty-two inches thick, strengthened
at the angles by stakes driven firmly into the
ground.

Fancy the rage of the South-Enders the next
day, when they spied our snowy citadel, with
Jack Harris's red silk pocket-handkerchief floating defiantly from the flagstaff.

In less than an hour it was known all over
town, in military circles at least, that the
"puddle-dockers" and the "river-rats" (these
were the derisive sub-titles bestowed on our
South End foes) intended to attack the fort that
Saturday afternoon.

At two o'clock all the fighting boys of the
Temple Grammar School, and as many recruits
as we could muster, lay behind the walls of Fort
Slatter, with three hundred compact snowballs
piled up in pyramids, awaiting the approach of
the enemy. The enemy was not slow in making
his approach—fifty strong, headed by one Mat
Ames. Our forces were under the command of
General J. Harris.

Before the action commenced a meeting was
arranged between the rival commanders, who
drew up and signed certain rules and regulations
respecting the conduct of the battle. As it was
impossible for the North-Enders to occupy the
fort permanently, it was stipulated that the
South-Enders should assault it only on Wednesday and Saturday afternoons between the hours
of two and six. For them to take possession of
the place at any other time was not to constitute
a capture, but, on the contrary, was to be considered a dishonorable and cowardly act.

The North-Enders, on the other hand, agreed

to give up the fort whenever ten of the storming party succeeded in obtaining at one time a footing on the parapet, and were able to hold the same for the space of two minutes. Both sides were to abstain from putting pebbles into their snowballs, nor was it permissible to use frozen ammunition. A snowball soaked in water and left out to cool was a projectile which in previous years had been resorted to with disastrous results.

These preliminaries settled, the commanders retired to their respective corps. The interview had taken place on the hillside between the opposing lines.

General Harris divided his men into two bodies; the first comprized the most skilful marksmen, or gunners; the second, the reserve force, was composed of the strongest boys, whose duty it was to repel the scaling parties, and to make occasional sallies for the purpose of capturing prisoners, who were bound by the articles of treaty to faithfully serve under our flag until they were exchanged at the close of the day.

The repellers were called light infantry; but when they carried on the operations beyond the fort they became cavalry. It was also their duty, when not otherwise engaged, to manufacture snowballs. The General's staff consisted of five Templars (I among the number, with the rank of major), who carried the General's orders and looked after the wounded.

General Mat Ames, a veteran commander, was no less wide-awake in the disposition of his army. Five companies, each numbering but six men, in order not to present too big a target to our sharpshooters, were to charge the fort from different points, their advance being covered by a heavy fire from the gunners posted in the rear. Each scaler was provided with only two rounds of ammunition, which were not to be used until he had mounted the breastwork and could deliver his shots on our heads.

The thrilling moment had now arrived. If I had been going into a real engagement I could not have been more deeply imprest by the importance of the occasion.

The fort opened fire first—a single ball from the dextrous hand of General Harris taking General Ames in the very pit of his stomach. A cheer went up from Fort Slatter. In an instant the air was thick with flying missiles, in the midst of which we dimly descried the storming parties sweeping up the hill, shoulder to shoulder. The shouts of the leaders, and the snowballs bursting like shells about our ears made it very lively.

Not more than a dozen of the enemy succeeded in reaching the crest of the hill; five of these clambered upon the icy walls, where they were instantly grabbed by the legs and jerked into the fort. The rest retired confused and blinded by our well-directed fire.

When General Harris (with his right eye bunged up) said, "Soldiers, I am proud of you!" my heart swelled in my bosom.

The victory, however, had not been without its price. Six North-Enders, having rushed out to harass the discomfited enemy, were gallantly cut off by General Ames and captured. Among these were Lieutenant P. Whitcomb (who had no business to join in the charge, being weak in the knees) and Captain Fred Langdon, of General Harris's staff. Whitcomb was one of the most notable shots on our side, tho he was not much to boast of in a rough-and-tumble fight, owing to the weakness before mentioned. General Ames put him among the gunners, and we were quickly made aware of the loss we had sustained by receiving a frequent artful ball which seemed to light with unerring instinct on any nose that was the least bit exposed. I have known one of Pepper's snowballs, fired point-blank, to turn a corner and hit a boy who considered himself absolutely safe.

But we had no time for vain regrets. The battle raged. Already there were two bad cases of black eye, and one of nose-bleed, in the hospital.

It was glorious excitement, those pell-mell onslaughts and hand-to-hand struggles. Twice we were within an ace of being driven from our stronghold, when General Harris and his staff leapt recklessly upon the ramparts and hurled the besiegers heels over head down hill.

At sunset the garrison of Fort Slatter was still unconquered, and the South-Enders, in a solid phalanx, marched off whistling "Yankee Doodle," while we cheered and jeered them until they were out of hearing.

III

ON RETURNING FROM EUROPE [3]

THIS page will be wafted possibly through a snow-storm to the reader's hand; but it is written while a few red leaves are still clinging to the maple bough, and the last steamer of the year from across the ocean has not yet discharged on our shores the final cargo of returning summer tourists. How glad they will be, like those who came over in previous ships, to sight that fantomish, white strip of Yankee land called Sandy Hook! It is thinking of them that I write.

Some one—that anonymous person who is always saying the wisest and most delightful things just as you are on the point of saying them yourself—has remarked that one of the greatest pleasures of foreign travel is to get home again. But no one—that irresponsible person forever to blame in railway accidents, but whom, on the whole, I vastly prefer to his garrulous relative quoted above—no one, I repeat, has pointed out the composite nature of this pleasure, or named the ingredient in it which gives the chief charm to this getting back. It is pleasant to feel the pressure of friendly hands once more; it is pleasant to pick up the threads of occupation which you dropt abruptly, or perhaps neatly knotted

[3] From Chapter IX of "From Ponkapog to Pesth." Copyright, 1883, by Thomas Bailey Aldrich. Published by Houghton, Mifflin Company.

together and carefully laid away, just before you stept on board the steamer; it is very pleasant, when the summer experience has been softened and sublimated by time, to sit of a winter night by the cheery wood fire, or even at the register, since one must make one's self comfortable in so humiliating a fashion, and let your fancy wander back in the old footprints; to form your thoughts into happy summer pilgrims, and dispatch them to Arles or Nuremberg, or up the vine-clad heights of Monte Cassino, or embark them at Vienna for a cruise down the swift Danube to Budapest. But in none of these things lies the subtle charm I wish to indicate. It lies in the refreshing, short-lived pleasure of being able to look at your own land with the eyes of an alien; to see novelty blossoming on the most commonplace and familiar stems; to have the old manner and the threadbare old custom to present themselves to you as absolutely new—or if not new, at least strange.

After you have escaped from the claws of the custom-house officers — who are not nearly as affable birds as you once thought them—and are rattling in an oddly familiar hack through well-known but half-unrecognizable streets, you are struck by something comical in the names on the shop signs—are American names comical, as Englishmen seem to think?—by the strange fashion of the iron lamp-post at the corner, by peculiarities in the architecture, which you ought to have noticed, but never did notice until now. The candid incivility of the coachman, who does not touch his hat to you, but swears at you, has the vague charm of reminiscence. You regard him as the guests regarded the poor relation at table in Lamb's essay; you have an impression that you have seen him somewhere before. The truth is, for the first time in your existence, you have a full, unprejudiced look at the shell of the civilization from which you emerged when you went abroad. Is it a pretty shell? Is it a satisfactory shell? Not entirely. It has strange excrescences and blotches on it. But it is a shell worth examining; it is the best you can ever have; and it is expedient to study it very carefully the two or three weeks immediately following your return to it, for your privilege of doing so is of the briefest tenure. Some precious things you do not lose, but your newly acquired vision fails you shortly. Suddenly, while you are comparing, valuing, and criticizing, the old scales fall over your eyes, and you insensibly slip back into the well-worn grooves, and behold all outward and most inward things in nearly the same light as your untraveled neighbor, who has never known

"The glory that was Greece
And the grandeur that was Rome."

You will have to go abroad again to renew those magical spectacles which enabled you for a few weeks to see your native land.

WILLIAM DEAN HOWELLS

Born in Ohio in 1837; consul to Venice in 1861-65; editor of *The Atlantic Monthly* in 1871-81; associate editor of *Harper's Magazine* since 1886; among his many works, "Venetian Life" published in 1866, "Italian Journeys" in 1869, "Poems" in 1867, "Their Wedding Journey" in 1872, "A Chance Acquaintance" in 1873, "The Lady of the Aroostook" in 1875, "The Undiscovered Country" in 1880, "A Modern Instance" in 1882, "Silas Lapham" in 1885, "Annie Kilburn" in 1888.

TO ALBANY BY THE NIGHT BOAT[1]

THERE is little proportion about either pain or pleasure: a headache darkens the universe while it lasts, a cup of tea really lightens the spirit bereft of all reasonable consolation. Therefore I do not think it trivial or untrue to say that there is for the moment nothing more satisfactory in life than to have bought your ticket on the night boat up the Hudson and secured your stateroom key an hour or two before departure, and some time even before the pressure at the clerk's office has begun. In the transaction with this castellated baron, you have, of course, been treated with haughtiness, but not with ferocity, and your self-respect swells with a sense of having escaped positive insult; your key clicks cheerfully in your pocket against its

[1] From Chapter III of "Their Wedding Journey." Copyright, 1871, 1888, Houghton, Mifflin Company.

gutta-percha number, and you walk up and down the gorgeously carpeted, single-columned, two-story cabin, amid a multitude of plush sofas and chairs, a glitter of glass, and a tinkle of prismatic chandeliers overhead, unawed even by the aristocratic gloom of the yellow waiters. Your own stateroom, as you enter it from time to time, is an ever new surprize of splendors, a magnificent effect of amplitude, of mahogany bedstead, of lace curtains, and of marble topt washstand. In the mere wantonness of an unalloyed prosperity you say to the saffron nobleman nearest your door, "Bring me a pitcher of ice-water, quick, please!" and you do not find the half-hour that he is gone very long.

If the ordinary wayfarer experiences so much pleasure from these things, then imagine the infinite comfort of our wedding journeyers, transported from Broadway on that pitiless afternoon to the shelter and the quiet of that absurdly palatial steamboat. It was not yet crowded, and by the river-side there was almost a freshness in the air. They disposed of their troubling bags and packages; they complimented the ridiculous princeliness of their stateroom, and then they betook themselves to the sheltered space aft of the saloon, where they sat down for the tranquiller observance of the wharf and whatever should come to be seen by them. Like all people who have just escaped with their lives from some menacing calamity, they were very philosophical in spirit; and having got aboard of their own motion, and being neither of them apparently the worse for the ordeal they had passed through, were of a light, conversational temper.

"What an amusingly superb affair!" Basil cried as they glanced through an open window down the long vista of the saloon. "Good heavens! Isabel, does it take all this to get us plain republicans to Albany in comfort and safety, or are we really a nation of princes in disguise? Well, I shall never be satisfied with less hereafter," he added. "I am spoiled for ordinary paint and upholstery from this hour; I am a ruinous spendthrift, and a humble three-story swell-front up at the South End is no longer the place for me. Dearest,

'Let us swear an oath, and keep it with an
    equal mind,'

never to leave this Aladdin's-palace-like steamboat, but spend our lives in perpetual trips up and down the Hudson."

To which not very costly banter Isabel responded in kind, and rapidly sketched the life they could lead aboard. Since they could not help it, they mocked the public provision which, leaving no interval between disgraceful squalor and ludicrous splendor, accommodates our democratic menage to the taste of the richest and most extravagant plebeian amongst us. He, unhappily, minds danger and oppression as little as he minds money, so long as he has a spectacle and a sensation, and it is this ruthless imbecile who will have lace curtains to the steamboat berth into which he gets with his pantaloons on, and out of which he may be blown by an exploding boiler at any moment; it is he who will have for supper that overgrown and shapeless dinner in the lower saloon, and will not let any one else buy tea or toast for a less sum than he pays for his surfeit; it is he who perpetuates the insolence of the clerk and the reluctance of the waiters; it is he, in fact, who now comes out of the saloon, with his womenkind, and takes chairs under the awning where Basil and Isabel sit. Personally, he is not so bad; he is good-looking, like all of us; he is better drest than most of us; he behaves himself quietly, if not easily; and no lord so loathes a scene. Next year he is going to Europe, where he will not show to so much advantage as here; but for the present it would be hard to say in what way he is vulgar, and perhaps vulgarity is not so common a thing after all.

JOHN HAY

Born in Indiana in 1838, died in 1905; graduated from Brown University in 1858; admitted to the bar in Illinois; one of the private secretaries of President Lincoln; secretary of Legation in Paris, Madrid and Vienna; Assistant Secretary of State in 1879-81; president of the International Sanitary Commission in 1891; ambassador to England in 1897-98; Secretary of State in 1898; author of "Castilian Days," published in 1871, "Pike County Ballads" in 1871, "Abraham Lincoln: a History," in collaboration with John G. Nicolay in 1890.

LINCOLN'S EARLY FAME [1]

HIS death seemed to have marked a step in the education of the people everywhere. It requires years, perhaps centuries, to build the structure of a reputation which rests upon the opinion of those distinguished for learning or intelligence; the progress of opinion from the few to the many is slow and painful. But in the case of Lincoln the many imposed their opinion all at once; he was canonized, as he lay on his bier, by the irresistible decree of countless millions. The greater part of the aristocracy of England thought little of him; but the burst of grief from the English people silenced in an instant every discordant voice. It would have been as imprudent to speak slightingly of him in London as it was in New York. Especially among

[1] From Volume X, Chapter XVIII, of "Abraham Lincoln: a History." Copyright, 1886, 1890, by John G. Nicolay and John Hay. Published by the Century Co.

the Dissenters was honor and reverence shown to his name. The humbler people instinctively felt that their order had lost its wisest champion.

Not only among those of Saxon blood was this outburst of emotion seen. In France a national manifestation took place, which the government disliked but did not think it wise to suppress. The students of Paris marched in a body to the American Legation to express their sympathy. A two-cent subscription was started to strike a massive gold medal; the money was soon raised, but the committee was forced to have the work done in Switzerland. A committee of French liberals brought the medal to the American minister, to be sent to Mrs. Lincoln. "Tell her," said Eugène Pelletan, "the heart of France is in that little box." The inscription had a double sense; while honoring the dead republican, it struck at the Empire: "Lincoln — the Honest Man; abolished Slavery, reestablished the Union; Saved the Republic, without veiling the Statue of Liberty."

Everywhere on the Continent the same swift apotheosis of the people's hero was seen. An Austrian deputy said to the writer, "Among my people his memory has already assumed superhuman proportions; he has become a myth, a type of ideal democracy." Almost before the earth closed over him he began to be the subject of fable. The Freemasons of Europe generally regard him as one of them—his portrait in masonic garb is often displayed; yet he was not one of that brotherhood. The spiritualists claim him as their most illustrious adept, but he was not a spiritualist; and there is hardly a sect in the

Western world, from the Calvinist to the atheist, but affects to believe he was of their opinion.

A collection of the expressions of sympathy and condolence which came to Washington from foreign governments, associations, and public bodies of all sorts, was made by the State Department, and afterward published by order of Congress. It forms a large quarto of a thousand pages, and embraces the utterances of grief and regret from every country under the sun, in almost every language spoken by man.

But admired and venerated as he was in Europe, he was best understood and appreciated at home. It is not to be denied that in his case, as in that of all heroic personages who occupy a great place in history, a certain element of legend mingles with his righteous fame. He was a man, in fact, especially liable to legend. . . .

Because Lincoln kept himself in such constant sympathy with the common people, whom he respected too highly to flatter or mislead, he was rewarded by a reverence and a love hardly ever given to a human being. Among the humble working people of the South whom he had made free this veneration and affection easily passed into the supernatural. At a religious meeting among the negroes of the Sea Islands a young man exprest the wish that he might see Lincoln. A gray-headed negro rebuked the rash aspiration: "No man see Linkum. Linkum walk as Jesus walk; no man see Linkum." . . .

The quick instinct by which the world recognized him even at the moment of his death as one of its greatest men, was not deceived. It has been confirmed by the sober thought of a quarter of a century. The writers of each nation compare him with their first popular hero. The French find points of resemblance in him to Henry IV; the Dutch liken him to William of Orange: the cruel stroke of murder and treason by which all three perished in the height of their power naturally suggests the comparison, which is strangely justified in both cases, tho the two princes were so widely different in character. Lincoln had the wit, the bonhomie, the keen practical insight into affairs, of the Béarnais; and the tyrannous moral sense, the wide comprehension, the heroic patience of the Dutch patriot, whose motto might have served equally well for the American President — "*Sævis tranquillus in undis.*" European historians speak of him in words reserved for the most illustrious names.

In this country, where millions still live who were his contemporaries, and thousands who knew him personally; where the envies and jealousies which dog the footsteps of success still linger in the hearts of a few; where journals still exist that loaded his name for four years with daily calumny, and writers of memoirs vainly try to make themselves important by belittling him— his fame has become as universal as the air, as deeply rooted as the hills. The faint discords are not heard in the wide chorus that hails him second to none and equaled by Washington alone. The eulogies of him form a special literature. Preachers, poets, soldiers, and statesmen employ the same phrases of unconditional love and reverence. Men speaking with the authority of fame use unqualified superlatives. . . .

It is not difficult to perceive the basis of this

sudden and world-wide fame, nor rash to predict its indefinite duration. There are two classes of men whose names are more enduring than any monument: the great writers, and the men of great achievement—the founders of states, the conquerors. Lincoln has the singular fortune to belong to both these categories; upon these broad and stable foundations his renown is securely built. Nothing would have more amazed him while he lived than to hear himself called a man of letters; but this age has produced few greater writers. We are only recording here the judgment of his peers. Emerson ranks him with Æsop and Pilpay, in his lighter moods. . . .

The more his writings are studied in connection with the important transactions of his age, the higher will his reputation stand in the opinion of the lettered class. But the men of study and research are never numerous; and it is principally as a man of action that the world at large will regard him. It is the story of his objective life that will forever touch and hold the heart of mankind. His birthright was privation and ignorance—not peculiar to his family, but the universal environment of his place and time; he burst through those enchaining conditions by the force of native genius and will: vice had no temptation for him; his course was as naturally upward as the skylark's; he won, against all conceivable obstacles, a high place in an exacting profession and an honorable position in public and private life; he became the foremost representative of a party founded on an uprising of the national conscience against a secular wrong, and thus came to the awful responsibilities of power in a time of terror and gloom. He met them with incomparable strength and virtue. Caring for nothing but the public good, free from envy or jealous fears, he surrounded himself with the leading men of his party, his most formidable rivals in public esteem, and through four years of stupendous difficulties he was head and shoulders above them all in the vital qualities of wisdom, foresight, knowledge of men, and thorough comprehension of measures. Personally opposed, as the radicals claim, by more than half of his own party in Congress, and bitterly denounced and maligned by his open adversaries, he yet bore himself with such extraordinary discretion and skill that he obtained for the government all the legislation it required, and so imprest himself upon the national mind that without personal effort or solicitation he became the only possible candidate of his party for reelection, and was chosen by an almost unanimous vote of the electoral colleges. . . .

To these qualifications of high literary excellence, and easy practical mastery of affairs of transcendent importance we must add, as an explanation of his immediate and world-wide fame, his possession of certain moral qualities rarely combined in such high degree in one individual. His heart was so tender that he would dismount from his horse in a forest to replace in their nest young birds which had fallen by the roadside; he could not sleep at night if he knew that a soldier-boy was under sentence of death; he could not, even at the bidding of duty or policy, refuse the prayer of age or helplessness in distress. Children instinctively loved him;

they never found his rugged features ugly; his sympathies were quick and seemingly unlimited. He was absolutely without prejudice of class or condition. Frederick Douglass says he was the only man of distinction he ever met who never reminded him, by word or manner, of his color; he was as just and generous to the rich and well-born as to the poor and humble—a thing rare among politicians. He was tolerant even of evil: tho no man can ever have lived with a loftier scorn of meanness and selfishness, he yet recognized their existence and counted with them. He said one day, with a flash of cynical wisdom worthy of a La Rochefoucauld, that honest statesmanship was the employment of individual meanness for the public good. He never asked perfection of any one; he did not even insist, for others, upon the high standards he set up for himself. At a time before the word was invented he was the first of opportunists. With the fire of a reformer and a martyr in his heart, he yet proceeded by the ways of cautious and practical statecraft. He always worked with things as they were, while never relinquishing the desire and effort to make them better. To a hope which saw the delectable mountains of absolute justice and peace in the future, to a faith that God in his own time would give to all men the things convenient to them, he added a charity which embraced in its deep bosom all the good and the bad, all the virtues and the infirmities of men, and a patience like that of nature, which in its vast and fruitful activity knows neither haste nor rest.

A character like this is among the precious

heirlooms of the republic; and by a special good fortune every part of the country has an equal claim and pride in it. Lincoln's blood came from the veins of New England emigrants, of Middle State Quakers, of Virginia planters, of Kentucky pioneers; he himself was one of the men who grew up with the earliest growth of the great West. Every jewel of his mind or his conduct sheds radiance on each portion of the nation. The marvelous symmetry and balance of his intellect and character may have owed something to this varied environment of his race, and they may fitly typify the variety and solidity of the republic. It may not be unreasonable to hope that his name and his renown may be forever a bond of union to the country which he loved with an affection so impartial, and served, in life and in death, with such entire devotion.

HENRY ADAMS

Born in Boston in 1838; graduated from Harvard in 1858; private secretary to his father, Charles Francis Adams, American Minister to England in 1861-68; a professor at Harvard in 1870-77; editor of the *North American Review* in 1870-76; author of "Essays in Anglo-Saxon Law," "Life of Albert Gallatin," and a "History of the United States" in nine volumes.

JEFFERSON'S RETIREMENT [1]

THE repeal of the embargo, which received the President's signature March 1, closed the long reign of President Jefferson; and with but one exception the remark of John Randolph was destined to remain true, that "never has there been any administration which went out of office and left the nation in a state so deplorable and calamitous." That the blame for this failure rested wholly upon Jefferson might be doubted; but no one felt more keenly than he the disappointment under which his old hopes and ambitions were crusht.

Loss of popularity was his bitterest trial. He who longed like a sensitive child for sympathy and love left office as strongly and almost as generally disliked as the least popular president who preceded or followed him. He had undertaken to create a government which should inter-

[1] From the final chapter of the "History of the United States in the Administration of Thomas Jefferson." Copyright, 1889, by Charles Scribners' Sons.

fere in no way with private action, and he had created one which interfered directly in the concerns of every private citizen in the land. He had come into power as the champion of state rights, and had driven states to the verge of armed resistance. He had begun by claiming credit for stern economy, and ended by exceeding the expenditure of his predecessors. He had invented a policy of peace, and his invention resulted in the necessity of fighting at once the two greatest powers in the world. . . .

In truth, the disaster was appalling; and Jefferson described it in moderate terms by admitting that the policy of peaceable coercion brought upon him mortification such as no other president ever suffered. So complete was his overthrow that his popular influence declined even in the South. Twenty years elapsed before his political authority recovered power over the Northern people; for not until the embargo and its memories faded from men's minds did the mighty shadow of Jefferson's Revolutionary name efface the ruin of his presidency. Yet he clung with more and more tenacity to the faith that his theory of peaceable coercion was sound; and when within a few months of his death he alluded for the last time to the embargo, he spoke of it as "a measure which, persevered in a little longer, we had subsequent and satisfactory assurance would have effected its object completely."

A discomfiture so conspicuous could not fail to bring in its train a swarm of petty humiliations which for the moment were more painful than the great misfortune. Jefferson had hoped to make his country forever pure and free; to abolish war with its train of debt, extravagance, corruption and tyranny; to build up a government devoted only to useful and moral objects; to bring upon earth a new era of peace and goodwill among men. Throughout the twistings and windings of his course as president he clung to this main idea; or if he seemed for a moment to forget it, he never failed to return and to persist with almost heroic obstinacy in enforcing its lessons. By repealing the embargo, Congress avowedly and even maliciously rejected and trampled upon the only part of Jefferson's statesmanship which claimed originality, or which in his own opinion entitled him to rank as philosophic legislator. The mortification he felt was natural and extreme, but such as every great statesman might expect, and such as most of them experienced. The supreme bitterness of the moment lay rather in the sudden loss of respect and consideration which at all times marked the decline of power, but became most painful when the surrender of office followed a political defeat at the hands of supposed friends. . . .

In his style of life as President, Jefferson had indulged in such easy and liberal expenses as suited the place he held. Far from showing extravagance, the White House and its surroundings had in his time the outward look of a Virginia plantation. The President was required to pay the expenses of the house and grounds. In consequence, the grounds were uncared for, the palings broken or wanting, the paths undefined, and the place a waste, running imperceptibly into the barren fields about it. Within, the house was as simple as without, after the usual style of Virginia houses, where the scale was often extravagant but the details plain. Only in his table did Jefferson spend an unusual amount of money with excellent results for his political influence, for no president ever understood better than Jefferson the art of entertaining; yet his table cost him no excessive sums. For the best champagne he paid less than a dollar a bottle; for the best Bordeaux he paid a dollar; and the Madeira which was drunk in pipes at the White House cost between fifty and sixty cents a bottle. His French cook and cook's assistant were paid about four hundred dollars a year. On such a scale his salary of twenty-five thousand dollars was equivalent to fully sixty thousand dollars of modern money; and his accounts showed that for the first and probably the most expensive year of his presidency he spent only $16,800 which could properly be charged to his public and official character. A mode of life so simple and so easily controlled should in a village like Washington have left no opening for arrears of debt; but when Jefferson, about to quit the White House forever, attempted to settle his accounts, he discovered that he had exceeded his income. Not his expenses as President, but his expenses as planter dragged him down. At first he thought that his debts would reach seven or eight thousand dollars, which must be discharged from a private estate hardly exceeding two hundred thousand dollars in value at the best of times, and rendered almost worthless by neglect and by the embargo. The sudden demand for this sum of money, coming at the moment of his political mortifications, wrung from him cries of genuine distress such as no public disaster had called out. . . .

On horseback, over roads impassable to wheels, through snow and storm, he hurried back to Monticello to recover in the quiet of home the peace of mind he had lost in the disappointments of his statesmanship. He arrived at Monticello March 15, and never again passed beyond the bounds of a few adjacent counties.

BRET HARTE

Born in 1839, died in 1902; removed to California in 1854, where in 1868 he founded *The Overland Monthly;* professor in the University of California in 1870; removed to New York in 1871; consul at Crefeld, Germany, in 1878-80, and at Glasgow in 1880-85; published "The Luck of Roaring Camp" in 1868, "The Outcasts of Poker Flat" in 1869, "Poems" in 1871, "Stories of the Sierras" in 1872, "Tales of the Argonauts" in 1875, "Gabriel Conroy" in 1876, "Two Men of Sandy Bar" (a play) in 1877, "A Phyllis of the Sierras" in 1888.

I

PEGGY MOFFAT'S INHERITANCE[1]

THE first intimation given of the eccentricity of the testator was, I think, in the spring of 1854. He was at that time in possession of a considerable property, heavily mortgaged to one friend, and a wife of some attraction, on whose affections another friend held an encumbering lien. One day it was found that he had secretly dug, or caused to be dug, a deep trap before the front door of his dwelling, into which a few friends in the course of the evening casually and familiarly dropt. This circumstance, slight in itself, seemed to point to the existence of a certain humor in the man, which might eventually get into literature; altho his wife's lover—a man of quick discernment, whose leg was broken by the

[1] From "The Twins of Table Mountain." Copyright, 1879, by Houghton, Mifflin Company.

fall—took other views. It was some weeks later that while dining with certain other friends of his wife, he excused himself from the table, to quietly reappear at the front window with a three-quarter-inch hydraulic pipe, and a stream of water projected at the assembled company. An attempt was made to take public cognizance of this; but a majority of the citizens of Red Dog who were not at dinner decided that a man had a right to choose his own methods of diverting his company. Nevertheless, there were some hints of his insanity: his wife recalled other acts clearly attributable to dementia; the crippled lover argued from his own experience that the integrity of her limbs could only be secured by leaving her husband's house; and the mortgagee, fearing a further damage to his property, foreclosed. But here the cause of all this anxiety took matters into his own hands and disappeared.

When we next heard from him, he had in some mysterious way been relieved alike of his wife and property and was living alone at Rockville, fifty miles away, and editing a newspaper. But that originality he had displayed when dealing with the problems of his own private life, when applied to politics in the columns of *The Rockville Vanguard* was singularly unsuccessful. An amusing exaggeration, purporting to be an exact account of the manner in which the opposing candidate had murdered his Chinese laundryman, was, I regret to say, answered only by assault and battery. A gratuitous and purely imaginative description of a great religious revival in Calaveras, in which the sheriff of the county—a notoriously profane skeptic—was alleged to have been the chief exhorter, resulted only in the withdrawal of the county advertising from the paper.

In the midst of this practical confusion he suddenly died. It was then discovered, as a crowning proof of his absurdity, that he had left a will, bequeathing his entire effects to a freckle-faced maid-servant at the Rockville Hotel. But that absurdity became serious when it was also discovered that among these effects were a thousand shares in the Rising Sun Mining Company, which a day or two after his demise, and while people were still laughing at his grotesque benefaction, suddenly sprang into opulence and celebrity. Three millions of dollars was roughly estimated as the value of the estate thus wantonly sacrificed. For it is only fair to state, as a just tribute to the enterprise and energy of that young and thriving settlement, that there was not probably a single citizen who did not feel himself better able to control the deceased humorist's property. Some had exprest a doubt of their ability to support a family; others had felt perhaps too keenly the deep responsibility resting upon them when chosen from the panel as jurors, and had evaded their public duties; a few had declined office and a low salary; but no one shrank from the possibility of having been called upon to assume the functions of Peggy Moffat the heiress.

The will was contested—first by the widow, who it now appeared had never been legally divorced from the deceased; next by four of his cousins, who awoke, only too late, to a consciousness of his moral and pecuniary worth. But the humble legatee—a singularly plain, unpretending, uneducated Western girl — exhibited a dogged pertinacity in claiming her rights. She rejected all compromises. A rough sense of justice in the community, while doubting her ability to take care of the whole fortune, suggested that she ought to be content with three hundred thousand dollars. "She's bound to throw even that away on some derned skunk of a man, natoorally; but three millions is too much to give a chap for makin' her onhappy. It's offerin' a temptation to cussedness."

The only opposing voice to this counsel came from the sardonic lips of Mr. Jack Hamlin. "Suppose," suggested that gentleman, turning abruptly on the speaker, "suppose, when you won twenty thousand dollars of me last Friday night—suppose that instead of handing you over the money as I did—suppose I'd got up on my hind legs and said, 'Look yer, Bill Wethersbee, you're a d—d fool. If I give ye that twenty thousand you'll throw it away in the first skin game in 'Frisco, and hand it over to the first short card-sharp you'll meet. There's a thousand—enough for you to fling away—take it and get!' Suppose what I'd said to you was the frozen truth, and you knowed it, would that have been the square thing to play on you?"

But here Wethersbee quickly pointed out the inefficiency of the comparison by stating that he had won the money fairly with a stake.

"And how do you know," demanded Hamlin savagely, bending his black eyes on the astonished casuist, "how do you know that the gal hezn't put down a stake?"

The man stammered an unintelligible reply.

The gambler laid his white hand on Wethersbee's shoulder.

"Look yer, old man," he said, "every gal stakes her whole pile—you can bet your life on that—whatever's her little game. If she took to keerds instead of her feelings, if she'd put up chips instead o' body and soul, she'd burst every bank 'twixt this and 'Frisco! You hear me?"

Somewhat of this idea was conveyed, I fear not quite as sentimentally, to Peggy Moffat herself. The best legal wisdom of San Francisco, retained by the widow and relatives, took occasion, in a private interview with Peggy, to point out that she stood in the quasi-criminal attitude of having unlawfully practised upon the affections of an insane elderly gentleman, with a view of getting possession of his property; and suggested to her that no vestige of her moral character would remain after the trial, if she persisted in forcing her claims to that issue. It is said that Peggy, on hearing this, stopt washing the plate she had in her hands, and twisting the towel around her fingers, fixt her small pale blue eyes on the lawyer.

"And ez that the kind o' chirpin' these critters keep up?"

"I regret to say, my dear young lady," responded the lawyer, "that the world is censorious. I must add," he continued, with engaging frankness, "that we professional lawyers are apt to study the opinion of the world, and that such will be the theory of—our side."

"Then," said Peggy stoutly, "ez I allow I've got to go into court to defend my character, I might as well pack in them three millions too."

There is hearsay evidence that Peg added to this speech a wish and desire to "bust the crust" of her traducers, and remarking that "that was the kind of hair-pin" she was, closed the conversation with an unfortunate accident to the plate, that left a severe contusion on the legal brow of her companion. But this story, popular in the bar-rooms and gulches, lacked confirmation in higher circles. . . .

The case came to trial. Everybody remembers it—how for six weeks it was the daily food of Calaveras County; how for six weeks the intellectual and moral and spiritual competency of Mr. James Byways to dispose of his property was discust with learned and formal obscurity in the court, and with unlettered and independent prejudice by camp-fires and in bar-rooms. At the end of that time, when it was logically established that at least nine-tenths of the population of Calaveras were harmless lunatics, and everybody else's reason seemed to totter on its throne, an exhausted jury succumbed one day to the presence of Peg in the courtroom. It was not a prepossessing presence at any time; but the excitement, and an injudicious attempt to ornament herself, brought her defects into a glaring relief that was almost unreal. Every freckle on her face stood out and asserted itself singly; her pale blue eyes, that gave no indication of her force of character, were weak and wandering, or stared blankly at the judge; her over-sized head, broad at the base, terminating in the scantiest possible light colored braid in the middle of her narrow shoulders, was as hard and uninteresting as the wooden spheres that topt the railing against which she sat. The jury, who for six weeks had had her described to them by the plaintiffs as an arch, wily enchantress, who had sapped the failing reason of Jim Byways, revolted to a man. There was something so appallingly gratuitous in her plainness that it was felt that three millions was scarcely a compensation for it. "Ef that money was give to her, she earned it sure, boys; it wasn't no softness of the old man," said the foreman. When the jury retired, it was felt that she had cleared her character; when they reentered the room with their verdict, it was known that she had been awarded three millions damages for its defamation.

She got the money. But those who had confidently expected to see her squander it were disappointed: on the contrary, it was presently whispered that she was exceeding penurious. That admirable woman Mrs. Stiver of Red Dog, who accompanied her to San Francisco to assist her in making purchases, was loud in her indignation. "She cares more for two bits than I do for five dollars. She wouldn't buy anything at the 'City of Paris' because it was 'too expensive,' and at last rigged herself out a perfect guy at some cheap slop-shops in Market Street. And after all the care Jane and me took of her, giving up our time and experience to her, she never so much as made Jane a single present." Popular opinion, which regarded Mrs. Stiver's attention as purely speculative, was not shocked at this unprofitable denouement; but when Peg refused to give anything to clear the mortgage off the new Presbyterian church, and even declined to take shares in the Union Ditch, considered by many as an equally sacred and safe investment, she began to lose favor. Nevertheless, she seemed to be as regardless of public opinion as she had been before the trial; took a small house, in which she lived with an old woman who had once been a fellow servant, on apparently terms of perfect equality, and looked after her money.

I wish I could say that she did this discreetly; but the fact is, she blundered. The same dogged persistency she had displayed in claiming her rights was visible in her unsuccessful ventures. She sunk two hundred thousand dollars in a worn-out shaft originally projected by the deceased testator; she prolonged the miserable existence of *The Rockville Vanguard* long after it had ceased to interest even its enemies; she kept the doors of the Rockville Hotel open when its custom had departed; she lost the cooperation and favor of a fellow capitalist through a trifling misunderstanding in which she was derelict and impenitent; she had three lawsuits on her hands that could have been settled for a trifle. I note these defects to show that she was by no means a heroine. I quote her affair with Jack Folinsbee to show she was scarcely the average woman. . . .

Nothing was known definitely until Jack a month later turned up in Sacramento, with a billiard cue in his hand, and a heart overcharged with indignant emotion.

"I don't mind saying to you gentlemen in confidence," said Jack to a circle of sympathizing players, "I don't mind telling you regarding this thing, that I was as soft on that freckle-faced, red-eyed, tallow-haired gal as if she'd been—a—a—an actress. And I don't mind saying, gentlemen, that as far as I understand women, she was just as soft on me. You kin laugh; but it's so. One day I took her out buggy-riding—in style too—and out on the road I offered to do the square thing, just as if she'd been a lady—offered to marry her then and there. And what did she do?" said Jack with a hysterical laugh. "Why, blank it all! offered me twenty-five dollars a week allowance — pay to be stopt when I wasn't at home!" The roar of laughter that greeted this frank confession was broken by a quiet voice asking, "And what did you say?" "Say?" screamed Jack, "I just told her to go to — with her money." . . .

During the following year she made several more foolish ventures and lost heavily. In fact, a feverish desire to increase her store at almost any risk seemed to possess her. At last it was announced that she intended to reopen the infelix Rockville Hotel, and keep it herself. Wild as this scheme appeared in theory, when put into practical operation there seemed to be some chance of success. Much doubtless was owing to her practical knowledge of hotel-keeping, but more to her rigid economy and untiring industry. The mistress of millions, she cooked, washed, waited on table, made the beds, and labored like a common menial. Visitors were attracted by this novel spectacle. The income of the house increased as their respect for the hostess lessened. No anecdote of her avarice was too extravagant for current belief. It was even alleged that she had been known to carry the luggage of guests to their rooms, that she might anticipate the usual porter's gratuity. She denied herself the ordinary necessaries of life. She was poorly clad, she was ill-fed—but the hotel was making money.

It was the particular fortune of Mr. Jack Hamlin to be able to set the world right on this and other questions regarding her.

A stormy December evening had set in when he chanced to be a guest of the Rockville Hotel. . . . At midnight, when he was about to retire, he was a little surprised however by a tap on his door, followed by the presence of Mistress Peg Moffat, heiress, and landlady of Rockville Hotel.

Mr. Hamlin, despite his previous defense of Peg, had no liking for her. His fastidious taste rejected her uncomeliness; his habits of thought and life were all antagonistic to what he had heard of her niggardliness and greed. As she stood there in a dirty calico wrapper, still redolent with the day's *cuisine*, crimson with embarrassment and the recent heat of the kitchen range, she certainly was not an alluring apparition. Happily for the lateness of the hour, her loneliness, and the infelix reputation of the man before her, she was at least a safe one. And I fear the very consciousness of this scarcely relieved her embarrassment. . . .

"I wanted to ask ye a favor about Mr.—about —Jack Folinsbee," began Peg hurriedly. "He's ailin' agin, and is mighty low. And he's losin' a heap o' money here and thar, and mostly to you. You cleaned him out of two thousand dollars last night—all he had."

"Well?" said the gambler coldly.

"Well, I thought as you woz a friend o' mine, I'd ask ye to let up a little on him," said Peg with an affected laugh. "You kin do it. Don't let him play with ye."

"Mistress Margaret Moffat," said Jack with lazy deliberation, taking off his watch and beginning to wind it up, "ef you're that much stuck after Jack Folinsbee, you kin keep him off of me much easier than I kin. You're a rich woman. Give him enough money to break my bank, or break himself for good and all; but don't keep him foolin' round me in hopes to make a raise. It don't pay, Mistress Moffat—it don't pay!" . . .

"When Jim Byways left me this yer property," she began, looking cautiously around, "he left it to me on conditions; not conditions ez waz in his written will, but conditions ez waz spoken. A promise I made him in this very room, Mr. Hamlin—this very room, and on that very bed you're sittin' on, in which he died."

Like most gamblers, Mr. Hamlin was superstitious. He rose hastily from the bed, and took a chair beside the window. The wind shook it as if the discontented spirit of Mr. Byways were without, reenforcing his last injunction.

"I don't know if you remember him," said Peg feverishly. "He was a man ez hed suffered. All that he loved—wife, fammerly, friends—had gone back on him. He tried to make light of it afore folks; but with me, being a poor gal, he let himself out. I never told anybody this. I don't know why he told me; I don't know," continued Peggy with a sniffle, "why he wanted to make me unhappy too. But he made me promise that if he left me his fortune, I'd never, never— so help me God!—never share it with any man or woman that I loved. I didn't think it would be hard to keep that promise then, Mr. Hamlin, for I was very poor, and hedn't a friend nor a living bein' that was kind to me but him.''

"But you've as good as broken your promise already," said Hamlin. "You've given Jack money, as I know."

"Only what I made myself. Listen to me, Mr. Hamlin. When Jack proposed to me, I offered him about what I kalkilated I could earn myself. When he went away, and was sick and in trouble, I came here and took this hotel. I knew that by hard work I could make it pay. Don't laugh at me, please. I did work hard, and did make it pay—without takin' one cent of the fortin'. And all I made, workin' by night and day, I gave to him; I did, Mr. Hamlin. I ain't so hard to him as you think, tho I might be kinder, I know.''

Mr. Hamlin rose, deliberately resumed his coat, watch, hat, and overcoat. When he was completely drest again, he turned to Peg.

"Do you mean to say that you've been givin' all the money you made here to this A1 first-class cherubim?"

"Yes; but he didn't know where I got it. O Mr. Hamlin! he didn't know that."

"Do I understand you that he's been bucking agin faro with the money that you raised on hash? and you makin' the hash?"

"But he didn't know that. He wouldn't hev took it if I'd told him."

"No, he'd hev died fust!" said Mr. Hamlin gravely. "Why, he's that sensitive that it nearly kills him to take money even of me."

II

JOHN CHINAMAN [2]

THE expression of the Chinese face in the aggregate is neither cheerful nor happy. In an acquaintance of half a dozen years, I can only recall one or two exceptions to this rule. There is an abiding consciousness of degradation — a secret pain or self-humiliation visible in the lines of the mouth and eye. Whether it is only a modification of Turkish gravity, or whether it is the dread Valley of the Shadow of the Drug through which they are continually straying, I can not say. They seldom smile, and their laughter is of such an extraordinary and sardonic nature—so purely a mechanical spasm, quite independent of any mirthful attribute—that to this day I am doubtful whether I ever saw a Chinaman laugh. A theatrical representation by natives, one might think, would have set my mind at ease on this point; but it did not. Indeed, a new difficulty presented itself—the impossibility of determining whether the performance was a tragedy or farce. I thought I detected the low comedian in an active youth who turned two somersaults, and knocked everybody down on entering the stage. But, unfortunately, even this classic resemblance to the legitimate farce of our civilization was deceptive. Another brocaded actor, who represented the hero of the play,

[2] From "The Luck of Roaring Camp." Copyright, 1871, 1899, Houghton, Mifflin Company.

turned three somersaults, and not only upset my theory and his fellow actors at the same time, but apparently ran amuck behind the scenes for some time afterward. I looked around at the glinting white teeth to observe the effect of these two palpable hits. They were received with equal acclamation, and apparently equal facial spasms. One or two beheadings which enlivened the play produced the same sardonic effect, and left upon my mind a painful anxiety to know what was the serious business of life in China. It was noticeable, however, that my unrestrained laughter had a discordant effect, and that triangular eyes sometimes turned ominously toward the "Fanqui devil"; but as I retired discreetly before the play was finished, there were no serious results. I have only given the above as an instance of the impossibility of deciding upon the outward and superficial expression of Chinese mirth. Of its inner and deeper existence I have some private doubts. An audience that will view with a serious aspect the hero, after a frightful and agonizing death, get up and quietly walk off the stage, can not be said to have remarkable perceptions of the ludicrous.

I have often been struck with the delicate pliability of the Chinese expression and taste that might suggest a broader and deeper criticism than is becoming these pages. A Chinaman will adopt the American costume, and wear it with a taste of color and detail that will surpass those "native, and to the manner born." To look at a Chinese slipper, one might imagine it impossible to shape the original foot to anything less cumbrous and roomy, yet a neater-fitting boot than that belonging to the Americanized Chinaman is rarely seen on this side of the continent. When the loose sack or paletot takes the place of his brocade blouse, it is worn with a refinement and grace that might bring a jealous pang to the exquisite of our more refined civilization. Pantaloons fall easily and naturally over legs that have known unlimited freedom and bagginess, and even garrote collars meet correctly around sun-tanned throats. The new expression seldom overflows in gaudy cravats. I will back my Americanized Chinaman against any neophyte of European birth in the choice of that article. While in our own State, the greaser resists one by one the garments of the Northern invader, and even wears the livery of his conqueror with a wild and buttonless freedom, the Chinaman, abused and degraded as he is, changes by correctly graded transition to the garments of Christian civilization. There is but one article of European wear that he avoids. These Bohemian eyes have never yet been pained by the spectacle of a tall hat on the head of an intelligent Chinaman.

My acquaintance with John has been made up of weekly interviews, involving the adjustment of the washing accounts, so that I have not been able to study his character from a social viewpoint or observe him in the privacy of the domestic circle. I have gathered enough to justify me in believing him to be generally honest, faithful, simple, and painstaking. Of his simplicity let me record an instance where a sad and civil young Chinaman brought me certain shirts with most of the buttons missing and others hanging on delusively by a single thread. In a moment of unguarded irony I informed him that unity would at least have been preserved if the buttons were removed altogether. He smiled sadly and went away. I thought I had hurt his feelings, until the next week, when he brought me my shirts with a look of intelligence, and the buttons carefully and totally erased. At another time, to guard against his general disposition to carry off anything as soiled clothes that he thought could hold water, I requested him to always wait until he saw me. Coming home late one evening, I found the household in great consternation over an immovable Celestial who had remained seated on the front door-step during the day, sad and submissive, firm but also patient, and only betraying any animation or token of his mission when he saw me coming. This same Chinaman evinced some evidences of regard for a little girl in the family, who in her turn reposed such faith in his intellectual qualities as to present him with a preternaturally uninteresting Sunday-school book, her own property. This book John made a point of carrying ostentatiously with him in his weekly visits. It appeared usually on the top of the clean clothes, and was sometimes painfully clasped outside of the big bundle of soiled linen. Whether John believed he unconsciously imbibed some spiritual life through its pasteboard cover, as the Prince in the "Arabian Nights" imbibed the medicine through the handle of the mallet, or whether he wished to exhibit a due sense of gratitude, or whether he hadn't any pockets, I have never been able to ascertain. In his turn he would sometimes cut marvelous imitation roses

239

from carrots for his little friend. I am inclined to think that the few roses strewn in John's path were such scentless imitations. The thorns only were real. From the persecutions of the young and old of a certain class his life was a torment. I don't know what was the exact philosophy that Confucius taught, but it is to be hoped that poor John in his persecution is still able to detect the conscious hate and fear with which inferiority always regards the possibility of even-handed justice, and which is the keynote to the vulgar clamor about servile and degraded races.

III

M'LISS GOES TO SCHOOL[3]

JUST where the Sierra Nevada begins to subside in gentler undulations, and the rivers grow less rapid and yellow, on the side of a great red mountain, stands "Smith's Pocket." Seen from the red road at sunset, in the red light and the red dust, its white houses look like the out-croppings of quartz on the mountain-side. The red stage topped with red-shirted passengers is lost to view half a dozen times in the tortuous descent, turning up unexpectedly in out-of-the-way places, and vanishing altogether within a hundred yards of the town. It is probably owing

[3] From M'Liss, one of the stories in "The Luck of Roaring Camp" volume. Copyright, 1871, 1899. Houghton, Mifflin Company.

to this sudden twist in the road that the advent of a stranger at Smith's Pocket is usually attended with a peculiar circumstance. Dismounting from the vehicle at the stage office, the too confident traveler is apt to walk straight out of town under the impression that it lies in quite another direction. It is related that one of the tunnelmen, two miles from town, met one of these self-reliant passengers with a carpet-bag, umbrella, *Harper's Magazine,* and other evidences of "civilization and refinement," plodding along over the road he had just ridden, vainly endeavoring to find the settlement of Smith's Pocket.

An observant traveler might have found some compensation for his disappointment in the weird aspect of that vicinity. There were huge fissures on the hillside, and displacements of the red soil, resembling more the chaos of some primary elemental upheaval than the work of man; while, half-way down, a long flume straddled its narrow body and disproportionate legs over the chasm, like an enormous fossil of some forgotten antediluvian. At every step smaller ditches crossed the road, hiding in their sallow depths unlovely streams that crept away to a clandestine union with the great yellow torrent below, and here and there were the ruins of some cabin with the chimney alone left intact and the hearthstone open to the skies.

The settlement of Smith's Pocket owed its origin to the finding of a "pocket" on its site by a veritable Smith. Five thousand dollars were taken out of it in one half-hour by Smith. Three thousand dollars were expended by Smith and others in erecting a flume and in tunnelling. And then Smith's Pocket was found to be only a pocket, and subject, like other pockets, to depletion. Altho Smith pierced the bowels of the great red mountain, that five thousand dollars was the first and last return of his labor. The mountain grew reticent of its golden secrets, and the flume steadily ebbed away the remainder of Smith's fortune. Then Smith went into quartz-mining; then into quartz-milling; then into hydraulics and ditching, and then by easy degrees into saloon-keeping. Presently it was whispered that Smith was drinking a great deal; then it was known that Smith was a habitual drunkard, and then people began to think, as they are apt to, that he had never been anything else. But the settlement of Smith's Pocket, like that of most discoveries, was happily not dependent on the fortune of its pioneer, and other parties projected tunnels and found pockets. So Smith's pocket became a settlement with its two fancy stores, its two hotels, its one express office, and its two first families. Occasionally its one long straggling street was overawed by the assumption of the latest San Francisco fashions, imported per express, exclusively to the first families; making outraged Nature, in the ragged outline of her furrowed surface, look still more homely, and putting personal insult on that greater portion of the population to whom the Sabbath, with a change of linen, brought merely the necessity of cleanliness, without the luxury of adornment. Then there was a Methodist church, and hard by a Monte bank, and a little beyond, on the mountain-side, a graveyard; and then a little schoolhouse.

"The Master," as he was known to his little flock, sat alone one night in the school-house, with some open copy-books before him, carefully making those bold and full characters which are supposed to combine the extremes of chirographical and moral excellence, and had got as far as "Riches are deceitful," and was elaborating the noun with an insincerity of flourish that was quite in the spirit of his text, when he heard a gentle tapping. The woodpeckers had been busy about the roof during the day, and the noise did not disturb his work. But the opening of the door, and the tapping continuing from the inside, caused him to look up. He was slightly startled by the figure of a young girl, dirty and shabbily clad. Still her great black eyes, her coarse, uncombed, lusterless black hair falling over her sun-burned face, her red arms and feet streaked with the red soil, were all familiar to him. It was Melissa Smith—Smith's motherless child.

"What can she want here?" thought the master. Everybody knew "M'liss," as she was called, throughout the length and height of Red Mountain. Everybody knew her as an incorrigible girl. Her fierce, ungovernable disposition, her mad freaks and lawless character were in their way as proverbial as the story of her father's weaknesses, and as philosophically accepted by the townsfolk. She wrangled with and fought the schoolboys with keener invective and quite as powerful arm. She followed the trails with a woodman's craft, and the master had met her before, miles away, shoeless, stockingless, and bareheaded, on the mountain road. The miners' camps along the stream supplied her with subsistence during these voluntary pilgrimages, in freely offered alms. Not but that a larger protection had been previously extended to M'liss. The Rev. Joshua McSnagley, "stated" preacher, had placed her in the hotel as servant, by way of preliminary refinement, and had introduced her to his scholars at Sunday school. But she threw plates occasionally at the landlord, and quickly retorted to the cheap witticisms of the guests, and created in the Sabbath school a sensation that was so inimical to the orthodox dulness and placidity of that institution, that, with a decent regard for the starched frocks and unblemished morals of the two pink-and-white-faced children of the first families, the reverend gentleman had her ignominiously expelled. Such were the antecedents, and such the character of M'liss, as she stood before the master. It was shown in the ragged dress, the unkempt hair, and bleeding feet, and asked his pity. It flashed from her black, fearless eyes, and commanded his respect.

"I come here to-night," she said rapidly and boldly, keeping her hard glance on his, "because I knew you was alone. I wouldn't come here when them gals was here. I hate 'em and they hates me. That's why. You keep school, don't you? I want to be teached!"

If to the shabbiness of her apparel and uncomeliness of her tangled hair and dirty face she had added the humility of tears, the master would have extended to her the usual moiety of pity, and nothing more. But with the natural, tho illogical instincts of his species, her boldness awakened in him something of that respect which all original natures pay unconsciously to one another in any grade. And he gazed at her the more fixedly as she went on still rapidly, her hand on that door-latch and her eyes on his:

"My name's M'liss—M'liss Smith! You can bet your life on that. My father's Old Smith— Old Bummer Smith—that's what's the matter with him. M'liss Smith—and I'm coming to school!"

"Well?" said the master.

Accustomed to be thwarted and opposed, often wantonly and cruelly, for no other purpose than to excite the violent impulses of her nature, the master's phlegm evidently took her by surprize. She stopt; she began to twist a lock of her hair between her fingers; and the rigid line of upper lip, drawn over the wicked little teeth, relaxed and quivered slightly. Then her eyes dropt, and something like a blush struggled up to her cheek, and tried to assert itself through the splashes of redder soil, and the sunburn of years. Suddenly she threw herself forward, calling on God to strike her dead, and fell quite weak and helpless, with her face on the master's desk, crying and sobbing as if her heart would break.

HENRY JAMES

Born in 1843; son of the elder Henry James; educated in
Europe; studied law at Harvard; began to write for periodi-
cals in 1866; has lived mostly in England since 1869; "A
Passionate Pilgrim" published in 1875, "The American" in
1877, "French Poets and Novelists" in 1878, "Daisy Miller"
in 1878, "Life of Hawthorne" in 1879, "Portrait of a Lady"
in 1881, "A Little Tour in France" in 1884, "The Boston-
ians" in 1886, "What Maisie Knew" in 1897, "The Awkward
Age" in 1899, "The Sacred Fount" in 1901.

I

AMONG THE MALVERN HILLS[1]

BETWEEN the fair boundaries of the counties
of Hereford and Worcester rise in a long undula-
tion the sloping pastures of the Malvern Hills.
Consulting a big red book on the castles and
manors of England, we found Lockley Park to
be seated near the base of this grassy range, tho
in which county I forget. In the pages of this
genial volume Lockley Park and its appurten-
ances made a very handsome figure. We took
up our abode at a certain little wayside inn,
at which in the days of leisure the coach must
have stopt for lunch, and burnished pewters of
rustic ale been tenderly exalted to "outsides"
athirst with breezy progression. Here we stopt,
for sheer admiration of its steep thatched roof,
its latticed windows, and its homely porch. We

[1] From "A Passionate Pilgrim and Other Tales." Copyright, 1875. Houghton, Mifflin Company.

allowed a couple of days to elapse in vague undirected strolls and sweet sentimental observance of the land, before we prepared to execute the especial purpose of our journey. This admirable region is a compendium of the general physiognomy of England. The noble friendliness of the scenery, its subtle old friendliness, the magical familiarity of multitudinous details, appealed to us at every step and at every glance. Deep in our souls a natural affection answered. The whole land, in the full, warm rains of the last of April, had burst into sudden perfect spring. The dark walls of the hedge-rows had turned into blooming screens; the sodden verdure of lawn and meadow was streaked with a ranker freshness. We went forth without loss of time for a long walk on the hills. Reaching their summits, you find half England unrolled at your feet. A dozen broad counties, within the vast range of your vision, commingle their green exhalations. Closely beneath us lay the dark, rich flats of hedgy Worcestershire and the copse-checkered slopes of rolling Hereford, white with the blossom of apples. At widely opposite points of the large expanse two great cathedral towers rise sharply, taking the light, from the settled shadow of the circling towns—the light, the ineffable English light! "Out of England," cried Searle, "it's but a garish world!"

The whole vast sweep of our surrounding prospect lay answering in a myriad fleeting shades the cloudy process of the tremendous sky. The English heaven is a fit antithesis to the complex English earth. We possess in America the infinite beauty of the blue; England possesses the splendor of combined and animated clouds. Over against us, from our station on the hills, we saw them piled and dissolved, compacted and shifted, blotting the azure with sullen rain-spots, stretching, breeze-fretted, into dappled fields of gray, bursting into a storm of light or melting into a drizzle of silver. We made our way along the rounded summits of these well-grazed heights—mild, breezy inland downs — and descended through long-drawn slopes of fields, green to cottage doors, to where a rural village beckoned us from its seat among the meadows. Close beside it, I admit, the railway shoots fiercely from its tunnel in the hills; and yet there broods upon this charming hamlet an old-time quietude and privacy, which seems to make it a violation of confidence to tell its name so far away. We struck through a narrow lane, a green lane, dim with its height of hedges; it led us to a superb old farm-house, now jostled by the multiplied lanes and roads which have curtailed its ancient appanage. It stands in stubborn picturesqueness, at the receipt of sad-eyed contemplation and the sufferance of "sketches." I doubt whether out of Nuremberg—or Pompeii!—you may find so forcible an image of the domiciliary genius of the past. It is cruelly complete; its bended beams and joists, beneath the burden of its gables, seem to ache and groan with memories and regrets. The short, low windows, where lead and glass combine in equal proportions to hint to the wondering stranger of the medieval gloom within, still prefer their darksome office to the grace of modern day.

Such an old house fills an American with an

indefinable feeling of respect. So propt and patched and tinkered with clumsy tenderness, clustered so richly about its central English sturdiness, its oaken vertebrations, so humanized with ages of use and touches of beneficent affection, it seemed to offer to our grateful eyes a small, rude synthesis of the great English social order. Passing out upon the highroad, we came to the common browsing-patch, the "village green" of the tales of our youth. Nothing was wanting; the shaggy, mouse-colored donkey, nosing the turf with his mild and huge proboscis, the geese, the old woman—the old woman, in person, with her red cloak and black bonnet, frilled about the face and double-frilled beside her decent, placid cheeks—the towering plowman with his white smock-frock, puckered on chest and back, his short corduroys, his mighty calves, his big, red, rural face. We greeted these things as children greet the loved pictures in a story book, lost and mourned and found again. It was marvelous how well we knew them. Beside the road we saw a plow-boy straddle, whistling on a stile. Gainsborough might have painted him. Beyond the stile, across the level velvet of a meadow, a footpath lay, like a thread of darker woof. We followed it from field to field and from stile to stile. It was the way to church. At the church we finally arrived, lost in its rook-haunted churchyard, hidden from the work-day world by the broad stillness of pastures—a gray, gray tower, a huge black yew, a cluster of village graves, with crooked headstones, in grassy, low relief. The whole scene was deeply ecclesiastical. My companion was overcome.

"You must bury me here," he cried. "It's the first church I have seen in my life. How it makes a Sunday where it stands!"

The next day we saw a church of statelier proportions. We walked over to Worcester, through such a mist of local color that I felt like one of Smollett's pedestrian heroes, faring tavernward for a night of adventures. As we neared the provincial city we saw the steepled mass of the cathedral, long and high, rise far into the cloud-freckled blue. And as we came nearer still, we stopt on the bridge and viewed the solid minster reflected in the yellow Severn. And going farther yet we entered the town—where surely Miss Austen's heroines, in chariots and curricles, must often have come a-shopping for swan's-down boas and high lace mittens; we lounged about the gentle close and gazed insatiably at that most soul-soothing sight, the waning, wasting afternoon light, the visible ether which feels the voices of the chimes, far aloft on the broad perpendicular field of the cathedral tower; saw it linger and nestle and abide, as it loves to do on all bold architectural spaces, converting them graciously into registers and witnesses of nature; tasted, too, as deeply of the peculiar stillness of this clerical precinct; saw a rosy English lad come forth and lock the door of the old foundation school, which marries its hoary basement to the soaring Gothic of the church, and carry his big responsible key into one of the quiet canonical houses; and then stood musing together on the effect on one's mind of having in one's boyhood haunted such cathedral shades as a King's scholar, and yet kept ruddy with much cricket in misty meadows by the Severn. On the third morning we betook ourselves to Lockley Park, having learned that the greater part of it was open to visitors, and that, indeed, on application, the house was occasionally shown.

Within its broad enclosure many a declining spur of the great hills melted into parklike slopes and dells. A long avenue wound and circled from the outermost gate through an untrimmed woodland, whence you glanced at further slopes and glades and copses and bosky recesses—at everything except the limits of the place. It was as free and wild and untended as the villa of an Italian prince; and I have never seen the stern English fact of property put on such an air of innocence. The weather had just become perfect; it was one of the dozen exquisite days of the English year—days stamped with a refinement of purity unknown in more liberal climes. It was as if the mellow brightness, as tender as that of the primroses which starred the dark waysides like petals wind-scattered over beds of moss, had been meted out to us **by the cubic** foot—tempered, refined, recorded!

II

TURGENEFF'S WORLD [2]

WE hold to the good old belief that the presumption, in life, is in favor of the brighter side, and we deem it, in art, an indispensable condition of our interest in a deprest observer that he should have at least tried his best to be cheerful. The truth, we take it, lies for the pathetic in poetry and romance very much where it lies for the "immoral." Morbid pathos is reflective pathos; ingenious pathos, pathos not freshly born of the occasion; noxious immorality is superficial immorality, immorality without natural roots in the subject. We value most the "realists" who have an ideal of delicacy and the elegiasts who have an ideal of joy.

"Picturesque gloom, possibly," a thick and thin admirer of M. Turgeneff's may say to us, "at least you will admit that it is picturesque." This we heartily concede, and, recalled to a sense of our author's brilliant diversity and ingenuity, we bring our restrictions to a close. To the broadly generous side of his imagination it is impossible to pay exaggerated homage, or, indeed, for that matter, to its simple intensity and fecundity. No romancer has created a greater number of the figures that breathe and move and speak, in their habits as they might have lived; none, on the whole, seems to us to have had such a masterly

[2] From "French Poets and Novelists," published by Macmillan & Company, of London.

touch in portraiture, none has mingled so much ideal beauty with so much unsparing reality. His sadness has its element of error, but it has also its larger element of wisdom. Life is, in fact, a battle. On this point optimists and pessimists agree. Evil is insolent and strong; beauty enchanting but rare; goodness very apt to be weak; folly very apt to be defiant; wickedness to carry the day; imbeciles to be in great places, people of sense in small, and mankind generally, unhappy. But the world as it stands is no illusion, no fantasm, no evil dream of a night; we wake up to it again for ever and ever; we can neither forget it nor deny it nor dispense with it. We can welcome experience as it comes, and give it what it demands, in exchange for something which it is idle to pause to call much or little so long as it contributes to swell the volume of consciousness. In this there is mingled pain and delight, but over the mysterious mixture there hovers a visible rule, that bids us learn to will and seek to understand.

So much as this we seem to decipher between the lines of M. Turgeneff's minutely written chronicle. He himself has sought to understand as zealously as his most eminent competitors. He gives, at least, no meager account of life, and he has done liberal justice to its infinite variety. This is his great merit; his great defect, roughly stated, is a tendency to the abuse of irony. He remains, nevertheless, to our sense, a very welcome mediator between the world and our curiosity. If we had space, we should like to set forth that he is by no means our ideal story-teller — this honorable genius possessing, attributively, a rarer skill than the finest required for producing an artful *réchauffé* of the actual. But even for better romancers we must wait for a better world. Whether the world in its higher state of perfection will occasionally offer color to scandal, we hesitate to pronounce; but we are prone to conceive of the ultimate novelist as a personage altogether purged of sarcasm. The imaginative force now expended in this direction he will devote to describing cities of gold and heavens of sapphire. But, for the present, we gratefully accept M. Turgeneff, and reflect that his manner suits the most frequent mood of the greater number of readers. If he were a dogmatic optimist we suspect that, as things go, we should long ago have ceased to miss him from our library. The personal optimism of most of us no romancer can confirm or dissipate, and our personal troubles, generally, place fictions of all kinds in an impertinent light. To our usual working mood the world is apt to seem M. Turgeneff's hard world, and when, at moments, the strain and the pressure deepen, the ironical element figures not a little in our form of address to those short-sighted friends who have whispered that it is an easy one.

END OF VOL. X

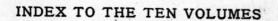

INDEX TO THE TEN VOLUMES

INDEX TO THE TEN VOLUMES

[Roman numerals indicate volumes, Arabic numerals indicate pages]

INDEX

INDEX

INDEX

INDEX

INDEX